HAVE YOU SEEN JESUS?

HAVE YOU SEEN JESUS?

by

David Johnson

Quality Publications
1-800-359-7708
P.O. Box 7385 • Fort Worth, TX 76111

TABLE OF CONTENTS

One	Have You Seen Jesus?	1
Two	Setting Priorities	9
Three	Humility and a Spirit of Service	17
Four	The Spirit of Compassion	25
Five	Misguided Zeal	31
Six	The Rebukes By Jesus Toward Others And Why They Occurred	39
Seven	Living In The World	47
Eight	Count The Cost	55
Nine	What Are You Doing For Christ?	63
Ten	Touching People Where They Hurt	69
Eleven	Those Who *Did* See Jesus	75
Twelve	The Faces of Jesus	85
Thirteen	What Have You Seen?	93

DEDICATION

This, my first book to be published, I lovingly dedicate to my parents, Willie and Martin Johnson. They lived and taught Christ before me always. They instilled in me the desire to learn and to constantly better myself. They made me believe I could do anything if I set myself to it. Without these traits this book would never have been born.

INTRODUCTION

As a child did you ever play with one of those toys (I think it's called a Kaleidoscope) that you would look through a hole on one end and turn the other end to see an unending variety of colorful designs? The slightest turn would cause you to see something new and different. Have you ever looked at a beautiful gem and noticed the different colors that can be seen within it just by a slight change in the angle in which you hold it?

This same principle is the basis for this book. Too often we don't look really close into the nature of Christ to really understand Him and His mission. We need to look from a different angle, a new viewpoint, with fresh insight to help us see Him as He truly was.

This book is the result of my reading A. T. Robertson's *A Harmony of the Gospels* one summer and trying to read it as if I didn't know anything about Jesus, but was trying to see Him for the first time. For every action Christ did, every response He made to someone, every parable He told I would ask myself, why did He do that? What was the purpose behind His action? What was He wanting to accomplish?

As a result, I began to see Jesus as I had never seen Him before. And I began to fear that I was not seeing Him in my life or the lives of other Christians the way He really was.

It is my hope that as you begin this study you will remove all preconceived ideas you have concerning Christ, His nature and His mission and you will enter into it prayerfully and thoughtfully. May you see our Savior as you have never before and may it make the same change in your life as it did in mine.

David Johnson

Chapter 1

HAVE YOU SEEN JESUS?

"And the disciples came and said unto him, 'Why speakest thou unto them in parables?' He answered and said unto them, 'Because it is given unto you to know the mysteries of the kingdom of heaven, but to them it is not given. For whosoever hath, to him shall be given, and he shall have more abundance: but whosoever hath not, from him shall be taken away even that he hath. Therefore speak I to them in parables: because they seeing see not; and hearing they hear not, neither do they understand. And in them is fulfilled the prophecy of Esaias, which saith, By hearing ye shall hear, and shall not understand; and seeing ye shall see, and shall not perceive: For this people's heart is waxed gross, and their ears are dull of hearing, and their eyes they have closed; lest at any time they should see with their eyes, and hear with their ears, and would understand with their heart, and should be converted, and I should heal them?" (Matthew 13:10-15).

Christ, in quoting Isaiah in the above passage, makes application to those who had seen Him but not fully understood His nature or mission. This was the ultimate reason for His rejection by the populace. Surely if they had truly "seen" Him, the majority would have gladly received Him. On close inspection of the books of Matthew, Mark, Luke, and John one is amazed at the number of people who did not see Jesus. As a matter of fact, if you made comparative lists of those who did see Jesus and those who did not see Him, the latter list would far surpass the prior one in length. And the saddest note concerning this is that all those who did not see Jesus as He really was actually thought they *did* see His true nature.

When there were so many who had literally been at the feet of Christ and thought they saw Him, but were mistaken, those who could have studied His life many times and didn't see Him is it not possible that we today think we see Christ but in reality we do not? Perhaps we have not tried hard enough to see His true nature and mission.

We begin this book on the life of Christ with the hope that you will study as if you had never heard of Jesus but are trying to see Him for the very first time. Look deeply and study slowly, trying to fathom the nature and mission of the Son of God.

This first chapter will focus on those who thought they saw Jesus but did not. Some in this chapter we are not surprised to find, others we are. The important question is, are we those who think we see Jesus but do not?

Herod the King

In Matthew chapter two we read of King Herod learning of the birth of Christ. Herod saw Him as a political threat, one who would grow up to lead an insurrection against the Roman government. This was Herod's motivation in ordering the senseless slaughter of the baby boys in Bethlehem.

Jesus' Friends From Nazareth

Mark relates to us in the 6th chapter the return of Christ to His homeland of Nazareth. "And when the sabbath day was come, he began to teach in the synagogue: and many hearing him were astonished, saying, 'From whence hath this man these things? and what wisdom is this which is given unto him, that even such mighty works are wrought by his hands? Is not this the carpenter, the son of Mary, the brother of James, and Joses, and of Juda, and Simon? and are not his sisters with us?' And they were offended at him."

These people saw Jesus only as a carpenter's son. They felt He should not be different from them.

The 5,000 Miraculously Fed

John 6 is the record of the wonderful miracle of Christ feeding the 5,000. The basic facts of the feeding are familiar enough to us. But even after witnessing this great miracle, the people do not see His true nature or mission. They determine to make Him an earthly king. "Then those men, when they had seen the miracle that Jesus did, said, 'This is of a truth that prophet that should come into the world.' When Jesus therefore perceived that they would come and take him by force, to make him a King, he departed again into a mountain himself alone." (vs. 14-15).

Their zeal was so great they crossed the sea the next day to again try to crown Jesus as their King (vs. 15-24).

Scribes in Capernaum

"When Jesus saw their faith, he said unto the sick of the palsy, 'Son, thy sins be forgiven thee.' But there were certain of the scribes sitting there, and reasoning in their hearts, 'Why doth this man thus speak blasphemies? who can forgive sins but God only?' " (Mark 2:5-7). These "spiritual leaders" saw Jesus as a trouble maker, one who blasphemed by placing Himself on an equal with God.

Pharisees in Jerusalem

John tells us of a remarkable conversation between Jesus and the Pharisees in Jerusalem (John 8:12-59). Read carefully these verses and notice that Jesus answers all their questions and accusations but they do not hear. They regard Him as one susceptible to suicide. "Will he kill himself?" They did not see He was from God. " 'Who art thou?' and Jesus saith unto them, 'Even the same that I said from the beginning.' And they understood not that he spake to them of the Father."

They saw Him as one who ridiculed their prized Jewish heritage (vs. 33-41).

Multitude in Jerusalem at Passover

Mark 11:1-11 and John 12:12-19 are parallel accounts of what we have come to refer to as the triumphal entry into Jerusalem. As Jesus approached, riding the donkey, "many spread their garments in the way: and others cut down branches off the trees, and strewed them in the way. And they that went before, and they that followed, cried, saying, 'Blessed is he that cometh in the name of the Lord: Blessed be the kingdom of our father David, that cometh in the name of the Lord.' "

But did these people really see Jesus? Why did they give Him this kind of reception? It was because they were expecting Him to crown Himself as their King and deliver them from the Roman rule.

The Apostles

"This beginning of miracles did Jesus in Cana of Galilee, and manifested forth his glory; and his disciples believed on him." (John 2:11). In this passage John makes it clear that he and the others believed on Christ from the beginning but he also makes it clear in verses 19-22 of that same chapter that they did not truly see His nature and mission until after He had resurrected following His death. "Jesus answered and said unto them, 'Destroy this temple, and in three days I will raise it up.' When therefore he was risen from the dead, his disciples remembered that he had said this unto them; and they believed the scripture, and the word which Jesus had said."

Let's take a chronological walk through the gospels and notice examples of the apostles not seeing.

In Luke 8:22-25 we find them amazed at Jesus' ability to calm a storm even though they had previously seen Him work other miracles. "And they being afraid wondered, saying one to another, 'What manner of man is this! for he commandeth even the winds and water, and they obey him.' "

In John 6 we see the apostles frantically searching for ways and means to feed the huge multitude of 5,000. They did not even consider the fact that Jesus could feed them.

Some time later the apostles are worried about feeding a crowd of 4,000 (Luke 8). "From whence can a man satisfy these men with bread here in the wilderness?" Again, they did not consider Christ's power.

Matthew 16:13-20 is the record of Peter making the good confession that Jesus Christ is the Son of God. But he shows that he does not understand Christ's nature and mission by immediately challenging the fact that Jesus must suffer and die (vs. 21-24). "Then Peter took him, and rebuked him, saying, 'Be it far from thee, Lord: this shall not be unto thee.' "

After the transfiguration (Mark 9), Peter, James, and John demonstrate they do not understand that Christ's mission involved His death, burial and resurrection. "And as they came down from the mountain, he charged them that they should tell no man what things they had seen, till the Son of man were risen from the dead. And they keep that saying with themselves, questioning one with another what the rising from the dead should mean."

Neither do the rest of the twelve yet understand His mission. "For he taught his disciples, and said unto them, 'The Son of man is delivered unto the hands of men and they shall kill him; and after that he is killed, he shall rise the third day.' But they understood not that saying, and were afraid to ask him." (Mark 9:30-32).

Even as Jesus approached Jerusalem for the last time, they did not see Him. "Then he took unto him the twelve, and said unto them, 'Behold, we go up to Jerusalem, and all things that are written by the prophets concerning the Son of man shall be accomplished. For he shall be delivered unto the Gentiles, and shall be mocked, and spitefully entreated, and spitted on: and they shall scourge him, and put him to death: and the third day he shall rise again.' And they understood none of these things: and this saying was hid from them, neither knew they the things which were spoken." (Luke 18:31-34).

In Mark 10:35-45 we see the apostles proving they do not understand the nature of Christ by arguing over who is to be the greatest in the kingdom, perhaps yet thinking, like others, that Jesus was to be an earthly King.

Just four days before the terrible ordeal of His trial and crucifixion and perhaps a couple of hours after Jesus had told His disciples of His impending death (Matthew 26:1-2), the disciples become indignant over a woman's anointing Jesus with costly oil (Matthew 26:6-13). They seem totally oblivious to who Jesus is or what He must suffer.

On Thursday, before Jesus' arrest, the apostles argue again over who is to be the greatest in the kingdom (Luke 22:24-30).

In a remarkable insight into Christ's understanding of this situation, He admits to Himself and the twelve that they still don't see Him, but He promises they will. "Now I tell you before it come, that, when it is come to pass, ye may believe that I am he." (John 13:13-19).

Even after seeing the empty tomb Peter and John did not understand who Christ really was. "For as yet they knew not the scripture, that he must rise again from the dead (John 20:1-10).

Conclusion

What was it that the people could not see about Jesus? They could not see that He was all powerful, that He must suffer and die, that He deserved to be treated with utmost honor and respect, that He was a servant to show the importance of service, that His kingdom was not of this world.

It is sad to consider that those who should have been the most prepared to see Him, the Jews, were the least prepared. And how ironic that those who were closest to the Saviour, the twelve, were so long in seeing Him.

Why did people have trouble seeing Jesus? It was due mainly to four reasons: (1) ignorance; (2) prejudice; (3) small thinking; (4) lack of faith.

People were ignorant of the true nature of the many prophecies concerning Christ. The prophecies were nearly always speaking in spiritual terms and the people were interpreting them in physical terms. Thus their expectance of an earthly kingdom.

The prejudice of many blinded their thinking and reasoning to the point of rejection. Most of the prejudice was linked to their ignorance. They had formed in their mind what the Saviour would be like and when Jesus did not fit their preconceived idea, they rejected Him.

The twelve were often guilty of small thinking. Did they think He could heal people but not feed them? Did they think He could feed 5,000 in one place and not 4,000 in another? Did they think He who could raise Lazarus from the dead could not Himself be raised up again? They were too involved in their own small lives, their concerns, their expectations to see the broadness of Christ's purpose.

When it came right down to it, most just simply could not believe that this man was the son of God the Father, come down from heaven, to live among men. It was too much for them to believe.

What about us? Do we really see Jesus? Hopefully the following chapters will help us see the true nature and mission of Jesus and cause us to avoid the mistakes of those in this chapter.

Lesson #1
Locate Where They Are Found

1. And they being afraid wondered, saying one to another, "What manner of man is this! for he commandeth even the winds and water, and they obey him." ____________________
2. "Hosanna: Blessed is the King of Israel that cometh in the name of the Lord." ____________________
3. And his disciples answered him, "From whence can a man satisfy these men with bread here in the wilderness?" ____________________
4. "Now I tell you before it came, that, when it is come to pass, ye may believe that I am he." ____________________
5. "Why does this man thus speak blasphemies? Who can forgive sins but God only?" ____________________
6. Philip answered him, "Two hundred pennyworth of bread is not sufficient for them." ____________________
7. When therefore he was risen from the dead, his disciples remembered that he had said this unto them; and they believed the scripture, and the word which Jesus had said. ____________________

8. For as yet they knew not the scripture, that he must rise again from the dead. ______

9. "Is not this the carpenter, the son of Mary, the brother of James, and Joses, and of Juda, and Simon?" ______

10. Then said the Jews, "Will he kill himself?" ______

Thought Questions

1. Are there people in the religious world today who do not see Jesus? Why do you answer as you do? ______

2. Are there people in the Church who do not see Jesus as He really is? ______

3. What are some misconceptions you think people have concerning Christ? ______

4. Are the reasons for their misconceptions different than those of the people of His day? ______

5. What is the only way to gain a proper understanding of Christ and His nature? ______

Chapter 2

SETTING PRIORITIES

(or, what things do you consider to be most important in your life?)

Have you ever sat down and thought about what things are most important in your life? Do you have a mental list of priorities for life? Probably most of us have not done these things. But we reveal our priorities every day by the things we do or don't do. Our actions show what we think is important or unimportant. When we say "yes" to one thing it is nearly always at the expense of saying "no" to something else. Therefore we are saying, "I think A is more important than B."

Let's look at five scenes in Christ's life where we can see individuals who were having trouble with their priorities or they had their priorities in the wrong place. Let's see if perhaps we can see our own tendencies reflected in these people and profit from their mistakes.

A Conversation With The Disciples

On one occasion, John 4, the disciples left Jesus to go in to Sychar to buy food. (While they were gone, Christ had His famous conversation with the Samaritan woman at the well.) Upon their return, the disciples were very concerned for Christ's physical welfare and urged Him to eat with them. "In the mean while his disciples prayed him, saying, 'Master, eat.' " (v. 31). Christ responds, v. 32, speaking in physical terms concerning spiritual things. "I have meat to eat that ye know not of." The disciples do not see the hidden meaning behind His words. They think He means someone has already given Him food. "Therefore said the disciples one to another, 'Hath any man brought him ought to eat?' " (vs. 33).

Jesus then expounds to them His meaning. "My meat is to do the will of him that sent me, and to finish his work. Say not yet, 'There are yet four months, and then cometh harvest?' behold, I say unto you, Lift up your eyes, and look on the fields; for they are white already to harvest. And he that reapeth receiveth wages and gathereth fruit unto life eternal: that both he that soweth and he that reapeth may rejoice together. And herein is that saying true, One soweth, and another reapeth. I sent you to reap that whereon ye bestowed no labour: other men laboured, and ye are entered into their labours." (vs. 34-38).

Christ is trying to show His disciples that they are more concerned with physical things, like eating and harvest time, than they are with spiritual things, like doing the will of the Father and harvesting souls. Each of us would do well to heed this same caution. Sometimes we are more concerned about working overtime on Sunday, to make time-and-a-half, than we are about worshipping God. Farmers are often guilty of being more concerned over harvesting their crops than they are over harvesting souls. Many of us don't put forth one-tenth the effort in saving souls that we put forth in saving things from our garden. Just where do our priorities lie?

A Conversation With The Pharisees

On another occasion the Pharisees challenged Christ because His disciples did not wash before eating. "Then came together unto him the Pharisees, and certain of the scribes, which came from Jerusalem. And when they saw some of the disciples eat bread with defiled, that is to say, with unwashen, hands, they found fault. For the Pharisees, and all the Jews, except they wash their hands oft, eat not, holding the tradition of the elders. And when they come from the market, except they wash, they eat not. And many other things there be, which they have received to hold, as the washing of cups, and pots, brasen vessels, and of tables. Then the Pharisees and scribes asked him, 'Why walk not the disciples according to the tradition of the elders, but eat bread with unwashen hands?" (Mark 7:1-5).

Jesus' first response to this charge is to condemn the Pharisees for practicing and teaching something that was not in the law. "Well hath Esais prophesied of you hypocrites, as it is written, 'This people honoureth me with their lips, but their heart is far from me.' Howbeit in vain do they worship me, teaching for doctrines the commandments of men. For laying aside the commandment of God, ye hold the tradition of men, as the washing of pots and cups: and many other such like things ye do." (vs. 6-8).

Christ then condemns them for their total lack of emphasis on the inside of man. "Harken unto me every one of you, and understand: There is nothing from without a man, that entering into him can defile him: but the things which come out of him, those are they that defile the man. If any man have ears to hear, let him hear" (vs. 14-16).

The disciples are slow to understand His message to the Pharisees so Christ explains this important principle to them. "Are ye so without understanding also? Do ye not perceive, that whatsoever thing from without entereth into the man, it cannot defile him; because it entereth not into his heart, but into the belly, and goeth out into the draught, purging all meats? That which cometh out of the man, that defileth the man. For from within, out of the heart of men, proceed evil thoughts, adulteries, fornications, murders, thefts, covetousness, wickedness, deceit, lasciviousness, an evil eye, blasphemy, pride, foolishness: all these evil things come from within, and defile the man" (vs. 18-23).

Aren't we today guilty of making the same mistake the Pharisees did? Focusing on the physical instead of the spiritual? We parents take so much pains and care in making sure our children are clean and dressed nice, but don't make any effort to nurture their soul. Everyone takes extra care to look nice before going to the worship services, but how many take time to prepare their heart for service through prayer and meditation? What are our actions saying about where our priorities are?

Another Conversation With The Disciples

Once again we are going to see the disciples making the mistake of focusing their thoughts and energies on physical things instead of spiritual. "Now the disciples had forgotten to take bread, neither had they in the ship with them more than one loaf." (Mark 8:14). Undoubtedly the disciples were frantic and embarrassed at the lack of preparation for their journey on the ship. Christ, knowing what was on their mind and hoping to direct their thoughts in another channel, said to them, "Take heed, beware of the leaven of the Pharisees, and of the leaven of Herod" (v. 15).

The disciples, with their minds already on the lack of food, "reasoned among themselves, 'It is because we have no bread' " (v. 16). They are so worried about physical sustenance, they do not try to look deeper in the words of the Saviour. Jesus, knowing they did not understand His meaning, "saith unto them, 'Why reason ye, because ye have no bread; perceive ye not yet, neither understand? have ye your heart yet hardened? Having eyes, see ye not? and having ears, hear ye not? and do ye not remember? When I brake the five loaves among five thousand, how many baskets full of fragments took ye up?' " (vs. 17-19). We can almost feel the frustration and exasperation on the part of Christ as He struggles to open the minds of these men. His challenge is, how can you imagine that I am concerned with physical bread when I have miraculously fed thousands? He continues to challenge them, "and when the seven among four thousand, how many baskets full of fragments took ye up?"

It would not be hard to imagine the disciples, under this severe questioning, to take on the appearance of a group of embarrassed school youngsters who have known the answer to an easy problem they were having trouble solving. No doubt the disciples were embarrassed to reply, "Twelve" and "Seven." The foolishness of their reasoning became all too apparent to them.

In one last stinging statement, designed to cause them to remember this lesson, Christ says, "How is it that ye do not understand?" (v. 22).

These disciples remind me of members of the church when they get together and start talking about the church. Or better yet, they remind me of some of the conversations that take place at the typical men's business meeting. "It's about time to paint the building again." "What color should we use?" "When are we going to stripe the parking lot?" "Someone needs to fix the light bulb out front." "The roof needs repairing." "Should we run the ceiling fans on high or low?"

Tragically, 90% of our time and energies are spent in physical areas and 10% (maybe) are spent in spiritual areas. We need to do some hard looking at our priorities.

Mary and Martha

"Now it came to pass, as they went, that he entered into a certain village: and a certain woman named Martha received him into her house. And she had a sister called Mary, which also sat at Jesus' feet, and heard his word. But Martha was cumbered about much serving, and came to him, and said, 'Lord, dost thou care that my sister hath left me to serve alone? Bid her therefore that she help me.' And Jesus answered and said unto her, 'Martha, Martha, thou are careful and troubled about many things: but one thing is needful: and Mary hath chosen that good part, which shall not be taken away from her.' " (Luke 10:38-42).

This story is very familiar to us. As we look at these two women it is obvious that the one who considered spiritual matters more important than physical matters was Mary. But how do we arrive at this conclusion concerning her? Does she say she is more interested in spiritual things?

No. We base our conclusion on her actions. Her actions reveal her priorities just as clearly as do Martha's actions reveal the importance she places on physical things.

As people look at our lives what do they see? What would our neighbors say are the most important things in our lives? Do our co-workers see us as more interested in physical things than spiritual things? What do our actions say about our priorities in life?

Jesus And A Synagogue Ruler

"And he was teaching in one of the synagogues on the sabbath. And behold, there was a woman which had a spirit of infirmity eighteen years, and was bowed together, and could in no wise lift up herself. And when Jesus saw her, he called her to him, and said unto her, ' Woman, thou art loosed from thine infirmity.' And he laid his hands on her: and immediately she was made straight, and glorified God. And the ruler of the synagogue answered with indignation, because that Jesus had healed on the sabbath day, and said unto the people, ' There are six days in which men ought to work: in them therefore come and be healed, and not on the sabbath day.' " (Luke 13:10-14).

This ruler of the synagogue, jealous of Jesus' power to heal and also of the attention and adoration the people gave to Jesus, hopes to disparage Christ's character by telling the people He has broken the law. Notice his comments were not directed to Christ but toward the people. Perhaps he had heard of Christ's ability to answer His accusers with unheard of skill. But this ruler was about to find out first hand what it was like to be "dressed down" in front of a crowd. Christ is going to lay bare this man's motives and reveal to all just where his priorities lie.

"The Lord then answered him, and said, 'Thou hypocrite, doth not each one of you on the sabbath loose his ox or his ass from the stall, and lead him away to watering? And ought not this woman, being a daughter of Abraham, whom Satan hath bound, lo, these eighteen years, be loosed from this bond on the sabbath day?' And when he had said these things, all his adversaries were ashamed: and all the people rejoiced for all the glorious things that were done by him." (vs. 15-17).

How humiliated this synagogue ruler must have felt! How foolish he looked in front of the people when it was revealed that he thought it all right to untie a donkey and give it water on the Sabbath but thought it wrong to release the sick from their diseases on the Sabbath. Such shallowness on his part as to the needs of people should be repulsive to us. He was so busy adhering to the letter of the law he forgot about caring for the people to whom the law was given.

Conclusion

I hope that as we have studied this lesson that we have seen the need in our lives to feel like the synagogue ruler and Christ's other adversaries—ashamed! To paraphrase Christ's words to Martha, "Brethren, brethren, we are careful and troubled about many things: but one thing is needful: and few hath chosen that good part which shall not be taken away from them."

Where are our priorities?

Lesson #2

Locate Where They Are Found

1. "My meat is to do the will of him that sent me, and to finish his work." ______
2. "Take heed, beware of the leaven of the Pharisees, and of the leaven of Herod." ______
3. "Martha, Martha, thou art careful and troubled about many things." ______
4. "Full well ye reject the commandment of God, that ye may keep your own traditions." ______
5. "And herein is that saying true, One soweth, and another reapeth." ______
6. "If any man have ears to hear, let him hear." ______
7. "There are six days in which men ought to work: in them therefore come and be healed, and not on the Sabbath Day." ______
8. "I have meat to eat that ye know not of." ______
9. "Lord, dost thou not care that my sister hath left me to serve alone?" ______
10. "Howbeit in vain do they worship me, teaching for doctrines the commandments of men." ______

Thought Questions

1. In the five scenes in the lesson what did the individuals consider most important in their life? ______

2. What things or criteria do people use to help them determine their priorities? ______________________________

____

3. What would be a good formula to use in setting one's priorities? ______

____

4. Are people in the Church more concerned about physical things or spiritual? Why? ______________________________

____

5. What are some things we sometimes put before our duty to Christ? ______

____

Chapter 3

HUMILITY AND A SPIRIT OF SERVICE

It would be very easy to develop two lessons on the subject of humility and a spirit of service. But is is hoped that the approach taken in this chapter of seeing these two traits as an outgrowth of each other and in a real sense as inseparable, will be an approach which will help us see this most important area of Christ's life.

No doubt Christ's humility was an easily recognizable trait and one of many that set Him apart from the common man. His entire life, from the lowly manger to the cruel cross, was one continuous day of humility. R. P. Meeks wrote, "Christ was of humble parentage, was born in humble circumstances, lived a humble life, associated with the humble and lowly, was the leader of the common people, and died the shameful death of the cross."

Let's notice four instances in which Christ emphasized the principles of humility and service.

Jesus Is Anointed By A Sinful Woman

"And one of the Pharisees desired him that he would eat with him. And he went into the Pharisee's house, and sat down to meat. And behold, a woman in the city, which was a sinner, when she knew that Jesus sat at meat in the Pharisee's house, brought an alabaster box of ointment, and stood at his feet behind him weeping, and began to wash his feet with tears, and did wipe them with the hairs of her head, and kissed his feet, and anointed them with the ointment. Now when the Pharisee which had bidden him saw it, he spake within himself, saying, 'This man, if he were a prophet, would have known who and what manner of woman this is that toucheth him: for she is a sinner.' And Jesus answering said unto him, 'Simon, I have somewhat to say unto thee.' And he saith, 'Master, say on.' There was a certain creditor which had two debtors: the one owed five hundred pence, and the other fifty. And when they had nothing to pay, he frankly forgave them both. Tell me therefore, which of them will love him most?' Simon answered and said, 'I suppose that he, to whom he forgave most.' And he said unto him, 'Thou hast rightly judged.' And he turned to the woman, and said unto Simon, 'Seest thou this woman? I entered into thine house, thou gavest me no water for my feet: but she hath washed my feet with tears, and wiped them with the hairs of her head. Thou gavest me no kiss: but this woman since the time I came in hath not ceased to kiss my feet. My head with oil thou didst not anoint: but this woman hath anointed my feet with ointment. Wherefore I say unto thee, her sins, which are many, are forgiven; for she loved much: but to whom little is forgiven, the same loveth little.' And he said unto her, 'Thy sins are forgiven.' And they that sat at meat with him began to say within themselves, 'Who is this that forgiveth sins also?' And he said to the woman, 'Thy faith hath saved thee; go in peace.' " (Luke 7:36-50).

Christ, the master teacher, seizes this opportunity, as He finds Himself in a setting of opposites in attitude, to teach an important lesson. One sees nothing that would indicate an attitude of humility on the part of Simon the Pharisee. What one does sense is an air of haughtiness in his attitude, especially when focusing on his attitude toward the sinful woman. This air of haughtiness comes across because we find him making no effort to be of service to his guest, Jesus. No kiss, no washing of feet, no anointing of oil, nothing that would give honor to his guest.

The logical question is why? If Simon had prepared a meal and invited a guest, why no actions to honor Him? It was due to his lack of humility. Perhaps he felt it beneath his dignity to do the things enumerated. In a moment we will notice that Simon's attitude did not go undetected by Jesus.

As we turn our attention to the actions of the sinful woman we see a total contrast in spirits. Here is a woman of deep humility with an eagerness to serve. One can almost see her humility deepen as in the presence of Christ she felt keenly her own sinful, lowly nature. As a result, there was no worthy action that she would have considered herself above performing.

Perhaps at first she came intending only to anoint His feet with oil (a common practice of that time). But that was not enough. She washed them with her tears, wiped them with her hair, and kissed them with her lips.

Christ uses this woman's actions as an opportunity to reveal the true nature of this man Simon, a lack of humility and willingness to serve. Perhaps at no other time had Simon taken a real good look at himself. But Christ lays his true spirit and motives bare before the entire crowd through the use of the parable and His words of praise toward the sinful woman.

The Disciples Argue Over Who Is To Be The Greatest

"At the same time came the disciples unto Jesus, saying, 'Who is the greatest in the kingdom of heaven?' And Jesus called a little child unto him, and set him in the midst of them, and said, 'Verily I say unto you, Except ye be converted, and become as little children, ye shall not enter into the kingdom of heaven. Whosoever therefore shall humble himself as this little child, the same is greatest in the kingdom of heaven. And whoso shall offend one of these little ones which believe in me, it were better for him that a millstone were hanged about his neck, and that he were drowned in the depth of the sea.' " (Matthew 18:1-6).

The one thing that the disciples argued over more than anything else was who was going to be greatest in importance in Christ's kingdom. The underlying cause of their arguing was a desire to be over someone else, to be able to *give* orders instead of *receiving* them, to be served instead of serving. They actually represent a perfect picture of the opposite of humility and a spirit of service.

Christ brings a little child to His arms and teaches these men two things: 1. They were not yet converted; 2. They needed to be more childlike, especially in humility.

The humility of children is reflected in their eagerness to learn and willingness to be taught. They readily recognize their dependence on others. Rarely do you find a child who thinks more highly of himself than he ought. It was these qualities in children that Christ wanted His disciples to see were lacking in their lives. And more importantly that their acceptance in the kingdom was dependent on their putting these things to practice in their lives. "Unless you change and become like little children, you will never enter the kingdom of heaven." (NIV).

The Disciples Receive Another Lecture on Humility

The setting for the following passage is, it is Thursday evening, perhaps just six or seven hours before the time Christ is to be arrested and begin the long ordeal that will lead to His death. Christ and His disciples have gathered to eat the Passover Meal.

"And there was also a strife among them, which of them should be accounted the greatest. And he saith unto them, 'The kings of the Gentiles exercise lordship over them; and they that exercise authority upon them are called benefactors. But ye shall not be so: but he that is greatest among you, let him be as the younger; and he that is chief, as he that doth serve. For whether is greater, he that sitteth at meat, or he that serveth? is not he that sitteth at meat? but I am among you as he that serveth. Ye are they which have continued with me in my temptations. And I appoint unto you a kingdom, as my Father hath appointed unto me; that ye may eat and drink at my table in my kingdom, and sit on thrones judging the twelve tribes of Israel.' " (Luke 22:24-30).

It is truly incredible and almost unbelievable that these twelve men, who had literally been living with Christ, could now, at the close of His brief life, find themselves arguing again over who is to be of greatest importance in the new kingdom! Perhaps the argument started over the seating arrangement at the meal. Each one arguing that he should be at the place of importance, the right hand of Christ. Trying to keep from sitting at the "foot" of the table.

It could be that the argument started over who should be the one to serve the meal. Each one thinking he deserved to be *served* along with Jesus instead of being the one serving the others. Each thinking, "I'm as good and important as the other disciples, why should I be the one to serve the meal?"

Perhaps the argument started over who should wash the feet of those present at the supper. (This we'll discuss in a moment.)

But regardless of what *triggered* the argument, the *cause* was a lack of humility and a spirit of service in the disciples' hearts.

Jesus tells them plainly that they are going to have to change. They should not desire lordship or authority over others or the seats of honor. They should show humility and be ready and eager to take the "back seat."

Christ also points out the importance of serving others. "If you want to be chief among my followers then *serve*." "Look at the example I have set for you. You consider me the greatest, yet I have eagerly served all men. Follow my example."

Christ Washes The Disciples' Feet

Our scene has not changed from our preceding point. Christ and His disciples are gathered and partaking of the Passover meal. It is probable that less than thirty minutes have passed since Christ spoke in Luke 22:30.

"He (Christ) riseth from supper, and laid aside his garments; and took a towel and girded himself. After that he poureth water into a basin, and began to wash his disciples' feet, and to wipe them with the towel wherewith he was girded. Then cometh he to Simon Peter: and Peter saith unto him, 'Lord, doest thou wash my feet?' Jesus answered and said unto him, 'What I do thou knowest not now; but thou shalt know hereafter.' Peter saith unto him, 'Thou shalt never wash my feet.' Jesus answered him, 'If I wash thee not, thou hast no part with me.' Simon Peter saith unto him, 'Lord not my feet only, but also my hands and my head.' Jesus saith to him, 'He that is washed needeth not save to wash his feet, but is clean ever whit: and ye are clean, but not all.' For he knew who should betray him; therefore said he, 'Ye are not all clean.' So after he had washed their feet, and had taken his garments, and was set down again, he said unto them, 'Know ye what I have done to you? Ye call me Master and Lord: and ye say well; for so I am. If then, your Lord and Master, have washed your feet, ye also ought to wash one another's feet. For I have given you an example, that ye should do as I have done to you. Verily, verily, I say unto you, The servant is not greater than his lord; neither he that is sent greater than he that sent him. If ye know these things, happy are ye if ye do them.' " (John 13:4-17).

The reason Jesus rose up during the meal was to drive home further the point He had just made in Luke 22. Even though Jesus spoke to them of humble service for others, still no one would swallow his pride enough to wash the feet of his fellow disciples. It is at this point that Jesus, probably thoroughly "put out" with His disciples, said to Himself, "If they will not *hear* my words maybe they will *see* them." Thus He rises and commences washing their feet.

No other single act in the history of mankind symbolizes more beautifully the true nature of humility and a spirit of service than does Jesus' actions here. When one pictures this scene he is reminded of the familiar words in Philippians 2:5-8, "'But made himself of no reputation, and took upon him the form of a servant, and was made in the likeness of men: and being found in fashion as a man, he humbled himself."

Can you imagine what thoughts must have gone through the minds of the disciples as He washed each one's feet?! What shame, embarrassment, foolishness, and humiliation they must have felt! It must have been quiet as death when Jesus finished and returned to His seat and asked them, "Do you understand what I have done for you?"

How much Jesus wanted these men to understand the importance of humility and a spirit of service! In essence He tells them, "If I, the very Son of God, whom you recognize as your Lord, or Ruler, and Teacher, wash your feet, then how much more ought you to wash each other's!" Commenting on this passage David Lipscomb wrote, "He (Christ) is enforcing on this occasion the greatest lesson of his mission—that the true end of the servant of God is to serve and not to be served, that men and angels will find their highest and best good in helping others. Man can bless himself only by blessing others."

Conclusion

The attitude of humble service for mankind is one of the most difficult for Christians to put into practice in their lives. We are like Simon the Pharisee, we invite Jesus into our lives and expect Him to serve us and us not serve Him. We all, like the disciples, let pride stand in our way too often. We see opportunities to serve but think, "Let someone else do it. I've got more important things to do." We want to do things that bring us honor and glory and praise of men. But, as Christ told His disciples, this should not be a part of our nature.

Solomon said, "Pride goeth before destruction, and a haughty spirit before a fall" (Proverbs 16:18). And notice that is exactly what happened to Simon the Pharisee! James wrote, "Humble yourselves in the sight of the Lord, and he shall lift you up" (James 4:10). With humility in our hearts we will be like the sinful woman and find no worthy action that we might consider ourselves above performing. Rather we will be ever searching for more ways to serve others.

A necessary part of our conversion is developing child-like humility that will be reflected in our eagerness to learn, willingness to be taught, and acknowledgement of our dependence on God. We must never get to the point that we feel we "know it all" and are unwilling to listen to others. And we must never think that we stand on our own two feet, "let him that thinketh he standeth take heed lest he fall" (1 Corinthians 10:12).

As David Lipscomb well said, "The true end of the servant of God is to serve and not to be served."

Lesson #3

Locate Where They Are Found

1. "This man, if he were a prophet, would have known who and what manner of woman this is that toucheth him: for she is a sinner." ____________________
2. "Whosoever therefore shall humble himself as this little child the same is greatest in the Kingdom of Heaven." ____________________
3. "Thy faith hath saved thee; go in peace." ____________________
4. 'If I then, your Lord and Master, have washed your feet; ye also ought to wash one another's feet." ____________________
5. "Her sins, which are many, are forgiven; for she loved much: but to whom little is forgiven, the same loveth little." ____________________
6. "Who is the greatest in the Kingdom of Heaven?" ____________________
7. "I am among you as he that serveth." ____________________
8. "Verily I say unto you, Except ye be converted and become as little children, ye shall not enter into the Kingdom of Heaven." ____________________
9. After he poureth water into a basin, and began to wash the disciples' feet, and to wipe them with the towel. ____________________
10. And there was also a strife among them, which of them should be accounted the greatest. ____________________

Thought Questions

1. In what ways are we like the disciples in Matthew 18:1-6? ____________________
2. Why did Christ praise the woman and not Simon in Luke 7:36-50? ____________________
3. Give some specific ways we can put to practice this attitude of humility and spirit of service in our family life. ____________________
4. Give some specific ways we can put to practice this attitude of humility and spirit of service in the Church. ____________________

5. Give some specific ways we can put to practice this attitude of humility and spirit of service in our job. ______________________
____
____

Chapter 4

THE SPIRIT OF COMPASSION

If there is one area in which we, as members of the church, fall short, as far as restoration of the 1st century church, it is the spirit of compassion. Webster defines compassion as "sympathetic consciousness of others' distress with a desire to alleviate it." Notice it is two-fold. Not just knowledge of need in the lives of others but a desire to alleviate that need.

One characteristic of Christ that impressed the people of His day and continues to impress people up to the present was His spirit of compassion. This spirit of compassion affected His dealing with people under varying circumstances. It shines brightly when contrasted with the seemingly total lack of compassion in the lives of the people of His day.

There are many scenes in Christ's life which show His compassionate spirit but we will focus on four that will show this spirit in a vivid way. Then we will notice the spirit of compassion commanded in the church of the 1st century. And finally we will see how we measure up as a people of compassion.

Jesus And The Samaritan Woman At The Well

In John the fourth chapter we have recorded a most remarkable conversation between our Saviour and a Samaritan woman. "Then cometh he to a city of Samaria, which is called Sychar, near to the parcel of ground that Jacob gave to his son Joseph. Now Jacob's well was there. Jesus therefore, being wearied with his journey, sat thus on the well: and it was about the sixth hour. There cometh a woman of Samaria to draw water: Jesus said unto her, 'Give me to drink.' " (v. 5-7).

The animosity felt between Jews and Samaritans was extremely intense and had existed since the return of the nation of Judah from Babylonian captivity. This hatred between the two people is verbalized by the woman's statement in verse 9, "How is it that thou, being a Jew, askest drink of me, which am a woman of Samaria?" The writer of the book then adds this comment, "for the Jews have no dealings with the Samaritans."

Thus we see Jesus' spirit of compassion already showing by not letting local prejudice keep Him from speaking to this Samaritan woman. His compassion is also seen in the manner in which He approached the subject of salvation with her. He began on common ground with a subject she could understand and relate to, that being thirst. Christ used a non-threatening approach to begin this most important conversation.

Jesus then continues the conversation, "If thou knewest the gift of God, and who it is that saith to thee, 'Give me to drink;' thou wouldest have asked of him, and he would have given thee living water."

The woman replies, "Sir, thou hast nothing to draw with, and the well is deep: from whence then hast thou that living water? Art thou greater than our father Jacob, which gave us the well, and drank thereof himself, and his children, and his cattle?"

Jesus was drawing a parallel between physical thirst and spiritual thirst. The Samaritan woman was having trouble following Him. But Jesus did not become impatient with her lack of understanding. He answered her, "Whosoever drinketh of this water shall thirst again: but whosoever drinketh of the water that I shall give him shall never thirst; but the water that I shall give him shall be in him a well of water springing up into everlasting life."

Jesus did not make this woman feel foolish or ignorant just because she could not understand Him. He did not condemn her for a lack of spirituality. Why? Because of the great compassion He had for this woman.

Jesus says to her, "Go, call thy husband, and come hither." The woman answers, "I have no husband." "Thou hast well said, 'I have no husband:', Jesus replies. "For thou hast had five husbands; and he whom thou now hast is not thy husband: in that saidst thou truly." (vs. 16-18).

The woman only told half the truth concerning her marriage relationship. Of course Jesus already knew the truth. Perhaps He wanted to test her honesty. Imagine her embarrassment at having been caught in this half truth! But Jesus does not condemn her for a lack of total honesty. He does not condemn her apparent adulterous relationship. Nor does He embarrass her or humiliate her. Why?! Because of His great compassion! And as a result, the conversation continues and this Samaritan woman hears the wonderful words of life.

Notice the result: "The woman then left her waterpot, and went her way into the city, and saith to the men, 'Come, see a man, which told me all things that ever I did: is not this the Christ?' " (vs. 28-29). "And many of the Samaritans of that city believed on him for the saying of the woman, which testified, 'He told me all that ever I did.' " (v. 39). "And many more believed because of his own word; and said unto the woman, 'Now we believe, not because of thy saying: for we have heard him ourselves, and know that this is indeed the Christ, the Saviour of the world.' " (vs. 41-42).

The spirit of compassion worked wonders in Samaria of old and it will work wonders in our society today.

Jesus Heals A Leper

"And there came a leper to him beseeching him, and kneeling down to him, and saying unto him, 'If thou wilt, thou canst make me clean.' And Jesus, moved with compassion, put forth his hand, and touched him, and saith unto him, 'I will; be thou clean.' And as soon as he had spoken, immediately the leprosy departed from him, and he was cleansed." (Mark 1:40-42).

What a tremendous picture of contrasts we have before us in this passage. A man with the most feared disease of that day beside He who had power over all diseases. A man undoubtedly scarred and disfigured by disease beside He who was perfect in every way. One man kneeling, another standing. One man begging, another granting.

The beauty of this scene is not only in the fact that Jesus paused to listen to this leper. Nor only in the fact that Jesus healed him. The beautiful part that shows Jesus' compassion is that Jesus "touched him." Jesus actually, physically touched this terribly diseased man. What is truly remarkable is that Jesus did not have to touch him in order to heal him. He could have just as easily spoken him clean. But Christ showed His compassion by doing that which perhaps no human being had done to this man for years! He touched him. Yes, Christ was truly a man with a compassionate spirit.

Jesus And The Adulterous Woman

The scribes and Pharisees were always testing Jesus and trying to trick Him. On this occasion they "brought unto him a woman taken in adultery; and when they had set her in the midst, they say unto him,

'Master, this woman was taken in adultery, in the very act. Now Moses in the law commanded us, that such should be stoned: but what sayest thou?' This they said, tempting him, that they might have to accuse him." (John 8:3-6).

Jesus' compassion for this woman, who was undoubtedly ashamed and embarrassed, caused Him to turn the tables on the scribes and Pharisees. "He said unto them, 'He that is without sin among you, let him first cast a stone at her.' " (v. 7). Now the scribes and Pharisees are embarrassed! The compassion of Jesus pointed out vividly to all those gathered around the total lack of compassion on the part of the scribes and Pharisees. These men left, being convicted by their own conscience. (v. 9).

When Jesus stands up and looks around, the only one left is the woman. Why didn't she run away when her accusers left? What would cause her to remain in Jesus' presence? She wanted to hear more from this man of compassion.

Jesus' compassionate spirit created a heart in this woman that could receive His instruction, "Go, and sin no more." (v. 11).

Jesus knew that this woman needed forgiveness not condemnation, help not ridicule, instruction not being cast aside.

Jesus And The Death Of A Friend

In John the eleventh chapter we have the record of the death of Lazarus. Some of Jesus' closest friends on this earth were Mary, Martha, and Lazarus. When Jesus learned of the death of Lazarus He determined to go there at great risk to His personal safety, that being the Jews were lying in wait for Him. Once again we see Jesus doing something that was not absolutely necessary. He could have spoken Lazarus back to life over the great distance but did not. Why?

His compassion for this dear family was such that He knew His personal presence would be a great comfort and encouragement to Mary and Martha. When Jesus saw the tear-stained face of Martha approaching Him, His first words to her were ones of hope and encouragement, "Thy brother shall rise again." (v. 23). He further comforts her with these words, "I am the resurrection, and the life: he that believeth in me, though he were dead, yet shall he live: and whosoever liveth and believeth in me shall never die." (vs. 25-26).

When Mary came crying to Him and, overwhelmed by her grief, falls at this feet, and when Jesus saw the other friends crying and grieving, He too was overwhelmed and wept. What great compassion! "Oh yes he cares! I know he cares! His heart is touched with my grief."—Frank E. Graeff

Compassion And The 1st Century Church

Now that we've noticed the spirit of compassion in the life of our Saviour, let's notice the command to those early Christians in the first century to keep that spirit of compassion alive in their lives. Jude speaks of the compassion to be had toward unbelievers who have not hardened their hearts to the truth. The KJV reads, "And of some have compassion, making a differencce." The ASV and NIV make the meaning more clear. "Be merciful to those who doubt" (Jude 22). This was exactly the course taken by Jesus toward the Samaritan woman. Here was a woman not used to thinking in spiritual terms. Jesus did not expect her to be able to grasp everything He said the first time He presented it to her, but through patience He helped her to grow in her understanding.

1 Peter 3:8 speaks of the compassion Christians are to have one toward another. "Finally, all of you, live in harmony with one another; be sympathetic, love as brothers, be compassionate and humble." (NIV). The unity and closeness felt by the members of the church in the first century was something that sustained them through all their persecutions and problems. The feeling of family, the desire for others to have the best, the willingness to forego one's own personal pleasure so that a brother or sister in Christ might prosper, all these characterized the church in its early existence.

Conclusion

Where has the spirit of compassion gone? Does the world see us as a compassionate people or a condemning people? What are we doing to let others know we care about them? Are we more eager to condemn than to convert? How do you feel about those outside the church? Do you feel eager to forgive them or condemn them? Are you searching for ways to help them or do you find yourself often ridiculing them? Do you search for ways and opportunities to patiently instruct them or do you feel "they're lost anyway, why try to reach them?"

What about the spirit of compassion toward our brothers and sisters in Christ? Do we do all we can to live in harmony with them? Are we sympathetic? Do we love our spiritual family as much as we love our physical family? How often do we treat each other with compassion and humility? Do you think the people in the congregation of which you are a member regard you as a person of deep compassion?

Let us offer this prayer to God in the hope we will focus more attention toward this area of our lives. "Father, help each of us to be more like your Son each day. And especially in the attitude of compassion. Help us to be looking for those who are in need and help us reach to them and show them Christ and thereby create in them a heart eager to hear the wonderful words of life. Through your Son we pray, Amen."

Lesson #4
Locate Where They Are Found

1. "God is a Spirit: and they that worship him must worship him in spirit and in truth." ______
2. "He that is without sin among you, let him first cast a stone at her." ______
3. "I am the resurrection, and the life." ______
4. "If thou wilt, thou canst make me clean." ______
5. "Whosoever liveth and believeth in me shall never die." ______
6. "How is it that thou, being a Jew, asketh drink of me, which am a woman of Samaria? for the Jews have no dealings with the Samaritans." ______
7. Jesus wept. ______
8. Finally, be ye all of one mind, having compassion one of another. ______
9. "Neither do I condemn thee: go, and sin no more." ______
10. And Jesus, moved with compassion, put forth his hand and touched him, and saith unto him, "I will; be thou clean." ______

Thought Questions

1. How would you define compassion? ______
2. Would you say that the majority of people in your community view you as a compassionate Church? Why or why not? ______
3. Give some specific way we can put into practice this spirit of compassion in our family life. ______
4. Give some specific way we can put into practice this spirit of compassion in our dealings with unbelievers. ______
5. Give some specific ways we can put into practice this spirit of compassion in our dealing with our brothers and sisters in Christ. ______

Chapter 5

MISGUIDED ZEAL

The word zeal is mentioned, in one form or another, in the Bible twenty-six times. Zeal means "eagerness and ardent interest in pursuit of something." Ardor is a synonym of zeal and it means "extreme vigor or energy." Other synonyms which help us understand better the word zeal are intensity and passion.

God's people in the first century were characterized by and encouraged to increase in their zeal. "For I know the forwardness of your mind, for which I boast of you to them of Macedonia, that Achaia was ready a year ago; and your zeal hath provoked very many." (2 Corinthians 9:2). "For I bear him record, that he hath a great zeal for you, and them that are in Laodicea, and them in Hierapolis." (Colossians 4:13). "Who gave himself for us, that he might redeem us from all iniquity, and purify unto himself a peculiar people, zealous of good works." (Titus 2:14). "As many as I love, I rebuke and chasten: be zealous therefore, and repent." (Revelation 3:19).

Thus we see that zeal is essential to christian living. But this chapter will center on a specific kind of zeal mentioned in Romans 10:2, misguided zeal. "For I bear them record that they have a zeal of God but not according to knowledge."

We will notice five instances in which Jesus had to deal with those who had misguided zeal. As we do we will notice what was the basic cause of this problem and Jesus' reaction to it.

Scribes and Pharisees

"And as he passed by, he saw Levi the son of Alphaeus sitting at the receipt of custom, and said unto him, 'Follow me.' And he arose and followed him. And it came to pass, that, as Jesus sat at meat in his house, many publicans and sinners sat also together with Jesus and his disciples: for there were many, and they followed him. And when the scribes and Pharisees saw him eat with publicans and sinners, they said unto his disciples, 'How is it that he eateth and drinketh with publicans and sinners?' " (Mark 2:14-16).

The scribes and Pharisees had misguided zeal toward publicans and sinners. Many publicans (tax collectors) were indeed corrupt, and they were regarded with much contempt and hatred because of the hardships they placed on the Jews. They were considered totally unworthy of even the slightest hint of spiritual help. The sinners who were gathered on this occasion were probably a mixed lot, including thieves, harlots, extortioners and such like. These too were regarded by the scribes and Pharisees as unworthy of help and perhaps beyond help.

The basic problem here is that the scribes and Pharisees could not disassociate sin from the sinner. Their utter contempt for sin led them to have utter contempt for the sinner. Indeed their zeal for hating sin is to be admired. We need more today who feel the same about sin. But Jesus teaches them, and at the same time us, a most important lesson. "They that are whole have no need of the physician, but they that are sick: I came not to call the righteous, but sinners to repentance." (v. 17).

A medical physician is one who is totally dedicated to wiping out disease. But we would consider a physician foolish indeed who refused to see sick people because he hated disease so much. By the same reasoning we, as Christians, are to dedicate our lives to destroying sin but we must not shrink away from those who are sinful. We cannot close our eyes to them and expect them to go away or get better on their own. We must expose them to the Balm of Gilead in order that their hearts might be healed. We must reach out to them just as Christ did: visit them in their homes; have them into our homes; let them know we care.

The Apostles

"And John answered him, saying, 'Master, we saw one casting out devils in thy name, and he followeth not us: and we forbad him, because he followeth not us.' " (Mark 9:38). The apostles became upset at a man working in the name of Jesus but one who was not following or belonging to their special group. They went so far as to forbid him from his work. They were motivated by good and honest reasons. They were eager and zealous to preserve these new truths they were learning from

Christ. They did not want anyone to mishandle or misrepresent the truth. A very admirable goal! But their actions were based on two false assumptions. One assumption was that they, the apostles, knew all the truth perfectly. And the other assumption was that no one who did not belong to their group could know the truth.

Jesus rebukes them for this attitude. "Forbid him not: for there is no man which shall do a miracle in my name, that can lightly speak evil of me. For he that is not against us is on our part. For whosoever shall give you a cup of water to drink in my name, because ye belong to Christ, verily I say unto you, he shall not lose his reward. And whosoever shall offend one of these little ones that believe in me, it is better for him that a millstone were hanged about his neck, and he were cast into the sea." (vs. 39-42).

Evidently here was a man who had embraced the teachings of Christ. Whoever was not against Christ was for Christ (v. 40). He was serving God in the best way he knew how. The apostles were treading on the dangerous ground of offending this "little one" and causing him to stumble. (v. 42).

We today must be so careful we do not exemplify this same attitude toward our brothers in Christ. In matters of opinion we must not deride, rebuke, and castigate others just because they do not hold the same opinions we do. We must allow others room in these areas.

James And John

"And it came to pass, when the time was come that he should be received up, he stedfastly set his face to go to Jerusalem, and sent messengers before his face: and they went, and entered into a village of the Samaritans, to make ready for him. And they did not receive him, because his face was as though he would go to Jerusalem." (Luke 9:51-53). Because Jesus had "set His face" or given clear indication that He was headed for Jerusalem, the Samaritans would not receive Him into their homes. Their action was prompted by the hatred all Samaritans had for Jews for not allowing them to have part in the service to God in Jerusalem after Judah returned from Babylonian captivity.

James and John took the Samaritans' action as a double offence. One, in that they were being rejected just because they were Jews. And two, in their rejection of Christ as the son of God. In their zeal for all to receive Jesus, James and John thought those who rejected Him were worthy only of swift and certain death. "And when his disciples James and John saw this, they said, 'Lord, wilt thou that we command fire to come down from heaven, and consume them, even as Elias did?" (v. 54).

But Jesus, no doubt to their amazement, rebuked them for their attitude. "But he turned, and rebuked them, and said, 'Ye know not what manner of spirit ye are of. For the Son of man is not come to destroy men's lives, but to save them.' " (vs.55-56). Jesus tells them that this vengeful attitude should not be part of their nature. They must learn patience and tolerance. The easy thing to do would have been to destroy the Samaritans with fire. The difficult task was to find ways to teach them and bring them to a better understanding of Christ's nature and mission. Jesus came with grace and mercy. And these are the traits all must practice.

As we go out into the world with the gospel we must be careful we don't shut doors of opportunity in the face of those who reject our initial efforts. The easy thing to do when someone rejects our efforts is to shrug our shoulders and say, "Forget them." The difficult task is to be more tolerant and patient with them and try to understand where they are coming from. Prayer, patience, and mercy may help us win them to Christ.

Lawyers And Pharisees

In the following scene Christ is at a large meal with the upper crust of society in Judea, that being lawyers and Pharisees. The Pharisees are known for their zeal concerning the performance of certain rituals (as noted in previous chapters). The Lawyers are known for their zeal concerning the letter of the law. But in this text we will find Christ blasting them with condemnations for their total lack of understanding of the concepts of love, humility, and good will that God desires in men.

"And as he spake, a certain Pharisee besought him to dine with him: and he went in, and sat down to meat. And when the Pharisee saw it, he marvelled that he had not first washed before dinner. And the Lord said unto him, 'Now do ye Pharisees make clean the outside of the cup and the platter; but your inward part is full of ravening and wickedness. Ye fools, did not he that made that which is without make that which is within also? But rather give alms of such things as ye have; and, behold, all things are clean unto you. But woe unto you, Pharisees! for ye tithe mint and rue and all manner of herbs, and pass over judgment and the love of God: these ought ye to have done, and not to leave the other undone. Woe unto you, Pharisees! for ye love the uppermost seats in the synagogue, and greetings in the markets. Woe unto you, scribes and Pharisees, hyprocrites! for ye are as graves which appear not, and the men that walk over them are not aware of them.'

"Then answered one of the lawyers, and said unto him, 'Master, thus saying thou reproachest us also.' And he said, 'Woe unto you also ye lawyers! for ye lade men with burdens grievous to be borne, and ye yourselves touch not the burdens with one of your fingers. Woe unto you! for ye build the sepulchres of the prophets, and your fathers killed them. Truly ye bear witness that ye allow the deeds of your fathers: for they indeed killed them, and ye build their sepulchres. Therefore also said the wisdom of God, I will send them prophets and apostles, and some of them they shall slay and persecute: and the blood of all the prophets, which was shed from the foundation of the world, may be required of this generation; from the blood of Abel unto the blood of Zacharias, which perished between the altar and the temple: verily I say unto you, it shall be required of this generation. Woe unto you, lawyers! for ye have taken away the key of knowledge: ye entered not in yourselves, and them that were entering in ye hindered.' " (Luke 11:37-54).

In their zeal for truth, the Pharisees and lawyers forgot about people. How sad! These men could have been the most effective tools available in the new kingdom. Their knowledge of the Old Law could have been a skillful tool in teaching others. But their misguided zeal rendered them worthless in that regard.

May God help us from making the same mistakes these lawyers and Pharisees made. May we never look at knowledge of the Bible as an end in and of itself. Knowledge of the Bible is a means of achieving an end result of saving ourselves and others. And let us not be hypocritical in binding things on others that we are not willing to bind on ourselves.

The Synagogue Ruler

This incident, Luke 13:10-17, was referred to back in chapter two. But don't let that dim your eagerness to read the text again. As with a precious jewel, when a text is turned and looked at from a different angle it often reveals previously unseen things. Ask yourself as you read the text, Why did the synagogue ruler act the way he did? What line of reasoning did he use to rebuke the actions of Jesus?

"And he was teaching in one of the synagogues on the Sabbath. And behold, there was a woman which had a spirit of infirmity eighteen years, and was bowed together, and could in no wise lift up herself. And when Jesus saw her, he called her to him, and said unto her, 'Woman, thou art loosed from thine infirmity.' And he laid his hands on her: and immediately she was made straight, and glorified God. And the ruler of the synagogue answered with indignation, because that Jesus had healed on the sabbath day, and said unto the people, 'There are six days in which men ought to work: in them therefore come and be healed, and not on the sabbath day.' "

This synagogue ruler was undoubtedly zealous to keep the Old Law. He even did an admirable thing, that is quote scripture. He recited a passage found in the book of Exodus. He assumed that quoting the Old Law would sufficiently put this trouble-maker, who healed on the Sabbath, in His place. But Jesus, in His response, shows the synagogue ruler's reasoning to be both inconsistent and false.

"Thou hypocrite, doth not each one of you on the sabbath loose his ox or his ass from the stall, and lead him away to watering? And ought not this woman, being a daugher of Abraham, whom Satan hath bound, lo, these eighteen years, he loosed from this bond on the sabbath?" The scripture the ruler had quoted had nothing to do with helping this woman's hurts. His zeal for the letter of the law blinded him to the needs of others and the opportunities to serve them.

Conclusion

Let it first be admitted and clearly stated, we must be a people who are zealous. Zealous of good works. But may we have the wisdom to learn from the mistakes of those noted in this chapter. Let's put to practice the things Christ tried to get them to see.

We must remember, misguided zeal can destroy our effectiveness.

Lesson #5

Locate Where They Are Found

1. Ye fools, did not he that made that which is without make that which is within also?" ______________________
2. "For the Son of man is not come to destroy men's lives, but to save them." ______________________
3. "And whosoever shall offend one of these little ones that believe in me, it is better for him that a millstone were hanged about his neck, and he were cast into the sea." ______________________
4. For I bear them record that they have a zeal of God, but not according to knowledge. ______________________
5. "Lord, wilt thou that we command fire to come down from heaven, and consume them, even as Elias did?" ______________________

6. And it came to pass, that, as Jesus sat at meat in his house, many publicans and sinners sat also together with Jesus and his disciples. ______________

____

7. "Woe unto you, Scribes and Pharisees, hypocrites! for ye are as graves which appear not, and the men that walk over them are not aware of them." ______________

8. "I came not to call the righteous, but sinners to repentance." ______________

____

9. "For he that is not against us is on our part." ______________

____

10. "They that are whole have no need of the physician, but they that are sick." ______________

Thought Questions

1. What is misguided zeal and why is it dangerous? ______________

____

2. What were some of the causes of misguided zeal we noted in this lesson? __

____

3. Apply these causes to our situation today. ______________

____

4. Can you relate an incident in which harm was done by someone with misguided zeal? ______________

____

5. How can we keep from having misguided zeal ourselves? ______________

____

Chapter 6

THE REBUKES BY JESUS TOWARD OTHERS AND WHY THEY OCCURRED

In the last two chapters we have noted the compassionate nature of our Saviour and His warning that we not be too quick to condemn and castigate others. Lest we develop a perception of Jesus as one who was never angry, never spoke a harsh word to anyone, but spoke only those things that were soothing and pleasing to His audience, we need to see another side of Jesus.

Some of the sharpest and most stinging words recorded in the Bible came from the lips of our Saviour. What was the nature of these rebukes? To whom were they directed? And why? What prompted the Christ, this most compassionate of men, to hurl rebukes that struck like lightning and shook like thunder? These are some questions we will answer as we look still deeper into the nature of Jesus.

"But I know you, that ye have not the love of God in you."

In John chapter 5 we read of Jesus' healing of a man who "had an infirmity thirty and eight years." Jesus told him, "Rise, take up thy bed, and walk." "And therefore did the Jews persecute Jesus, and sought to slay him, because he had done these things on the sabbath day." Jesus' answer to them was that He was simply doing the will of His Father. "Therefore the Jews sought the more to kill him, because he had not only broken the sabbath, but said also that God was his Father, making himself equal with God."

Christ's response is recorded in the last twenty-eight verses of this chapter. He first tells these Jews where He is from and from whom He receives power and authority. "The son can do nothing of himself, but what he sees the Father do." (vs. 19-36). He then attacks them and shows them to be totally lacking in the godliness they prided themselves in having. "And the Father himself which hath sent me, hath borne witness of me. Ye have neither heard his voice at any time, nor seen his shape. And ye have not his word abiding in you: for whom he hath sent, him ye believe not. Search the scriptures; for in them ye think ye have eternal life: and they are they which testify of me. And ye will not come to me, that ye might have life. I receive not honour from men. But I know you, that ye have not the love of God in you. I am come in my Father's name, and ye receive me not: if another shall come in his own name, him ye will receive. How can ye believe, which receive honor one of another, and seek not the honour that cometh from God only? Do not think that I will accuse you to the Father: there is one that accuseth you, even Moses, in whom ye trust. For had ye believed Moses, ye would have believed me: for he wrote of me. But if ye believe not his writings, how shall ye believe my words?" (vs. 37-47).

This was a stinging rebuke toward the Jews that they felt sharply. The Jews considered themselves to be more godly than anyone on the earth due to their lineage from Abraham. To even hint that they might not love god was to strike a blow at the very nature of their existence.

The Jews, more than any other people, should have been ready to receive Christ. All the prophecies in the Old Law concerning His coming were well known. The constant hope of every Jew was the coming of the Messiah. God had providentially protected their race for generations to provide for the coming of His son. Yet when Christ finally came they were not prepared. And this is why Jesus condemns them.

Woes Upon The Cities Of Chorazin, Bethsaida, and Capernaum

"Then began he to upbraid the cities wherein most of his mighty works were done, because they repented not: 'Woe unto thee, Chorazin! woe unto thee, Bethsaida! for if the mighty works, which were done in you, had been done in Tyre and Sidon, they would have repented long ago in sackcloth and ashes. But I say unto you, it shall be more tolerable for Tyre and Sidon at the day of the judgment, than for you. And thou, Capernaum, which art exalted unto heaven, shalt be brought down to hell: for if the mighty works, which have been done in thee, had been done in Sodom, it would have remained until this day. But I say unto you, that it shall be more tolerable for the land of Sodom in the day of Judgment, than for thee.' " (Matthew 11:20-24).

Christ had done some of His mightiest works, or miracles, in these cities, yet they had still rejected Him. Their belief in the face of undisputable testimony destined them to suffer unbelievable torment and prompted this fierce rebuke from our Lord.

"O Generation Of Vipers"

The Pharisees were the self-imposed watchdogs of orthodoxy. And on one occasion they accused Christ of receiving His power from the Devil himself. "Then was brought unto him one possessed with a devil, blind, and dumb: and he healed him, insomuch that the blind and dumb both spake and saw. And all the people were amazed, and said, 'Is not this the son of David?' But when the Pharisees heard it, they said, 'This fellow doth not cast out devils, but by Beelzebul the prince of the devils.' " (Matthew 12:22-24).

Jesus responds in part, "O generation of vipers, how can ye, being evil, speak good things?" (v. 34). How startled these men must have been to hear themselves called a viper, an animal despised by all mankind! They were "watchdogs" over something they actually knew nothing about. Jesus rebukes them for ascribing His power to the devil.

"This people honoureth me with their lips, but their heart is far from me."

In this setting, the Pharisees from Jerusalem condemn Jesus' disciples for eating with unwashed hands. (Mark 7:1-23). Fire must have flown from the eyes of Jesus as He turned on these Pharisees and accused them of having hearts far from God, of worshipping in vain, and of laying aside the commandments of God. Christ condemns them for their total lack of emphasis on the inside of man. "This people honoureth me with their lips, but their heart is far from me. Howbeit in vain do they worship me. . . laying aside the commandment of God. . . Full well ye reject the command of God. . . Making the word of God of none effect through your tradition."

"Have ye your heart yet hardened?"

Perhaps unexpectedly we find Jesus rebuking the chosen twelve. "Perceive ye not yet, neither understand? have ye your heart yet hardened? having eyes, see ye not? and having ears, hear ye not? and do ye not remember?" (Mark 8:17-18). These men, coming from a Jewish background, thought like the Jews, that is in physical terms. They were not focusing on spiritual things. Jesus rebukes them for this type of thinking and for their lack of spiritual growth.

"Ye are of your father the devil"

In John 8:21-59 we find Jesus, in a very patient manner, trying again to explain to the Jews and Pharisees who He is and that they should have been expecting Him. "Ye are from beneath; I am from above: ye are of this world; I am not of this world. . . When ye have lifted up the Son of men, then shall ye know that I am he, and that I do nothing of myself; but as my Father hath taught me, I speak these things."

He then points out to them that they should trust in Him and not in their heritage as children of Abraham. "I know that ye are Abraham's seed; but ye seek to kill me. . . If ye were Abraham's children, ye would do the works of Abraham. But now ye seek to kill me, a man that hath told you the truth, which I have heard of God: this did not Abraham."

Because of their prejudice they could not see Christ and He blasts them because they refuse to believe who He is. "Why do ye not understand my speech? even because ye cannot hear my word. Ye are of your father the devil, and the lusts of your father ye will do. . . And because I tell you the truth, ye believe me not."

"Martha, Martha!"

Christ's reprimand of Martha is found in Luke 10:38-42. The sting Martha felt from this reprimand was undoubtedly due in part to the fact that it was unexpected. She was busy fixing the meal and straightening the house. A worthy task. She probably expected Jesus to reprimand Mary for her apparent laziness. But Christ gently rebukes Martha for having too much interest in physical things instead of spiritual things. "Martha, Martha, thou art careful and troubled about many things: but one thing is needful: and Mary hath chosen that good part, which shall not be taken away from her."

"Woe unto you, Pharisees and lawyers!"

At a meal with the upper crust of society in Judea, lawyers, scribes, and Pharisees, Jesus blasts them with condemnation for their total lack of understanding the concepts of love, humility, and good will that God desires in man (Luke 11:37-54). He lashes out at the things they felt most strongly about: Washing; "Now do ye Pharisees make clean the outside of the cup and the platter; but your inward part is full of ravening and wickedness." Tithing; "But woe unto you, Pharisees! for ye tithe mint and rue and all manner of herbs, and pass over judgment and the love of God: these ought ye to have done, and not to leave the other undone." Seats of honor; "Woe unto you, Pharisees! for ye love the uppermost seats in the synagogues, and greetings in the markets."

"Thou hypocrite"

In Luke 13:10-17 Jesus rebukes a synagogue ruler because he thought it all right to untie his donkey and give it water on the sabbath, but thought it wrong to release the sick from their disease on the sabbath. Christ refers to this ruler as a "hypocrite."

The sharpness with which Christ's words cut this man was threefold. First, as a ruler of the synagogue he was not used to being challenged. He was used to being met with submission to his words of indignation. Second, he was humiliated by a common man, Jesus, in front of a crowd. How red his face must have become! Third, this ruler knew that Jesus spoke words of truth.

"He was much displeased"

In Mark 10:13-16 we read once again Jesus found it necessary to rebuke His disciples. "And they brought young children to him, that he should touch them: and his disciples rebuked those that brought them. But when Jesus saw it, he was much displeased, and said unto them, 'Suffer the little children to come unto me, and forbid them not: for of such is the kingdom of God. Verily I say unto you, whosoever shall not receive the kingdom of God as a little child, he shall not enter therein.' "

As much as Jesus loved these men and as much as He wanted to support them in all their decisions, He still, when necessary, would rebuke them to keep them on the straight and narrow.

Matthew 23

Perhaps no harsher language has been used before or since by mortal man to describe the terrible emptiness that was in the lives of men than that used by Jesus in the twenty-third chapter of Matthew. To appreciate even more this remarkable passage let's put it into the proper chronological context of events. On Tuesday, after Christ's triumphal entry into Jerusalem and before His arrest Thursday, Jesus uses three parables in causing the Sanhedrin to condemn themselves with their own words in front of the people (Matthew 21:23-22:14). Next Jesus answers a trick question by the Sadducees (Luke 20:27-40). Patiently, Jesus answers a Pharisee lawyer's legal question (Mark 12:28-34). Next, Jesus turns the tables and asks the Pharisees a question they cannot answer (Matthew 22:41-46). Then, drained of patience and filled with righteous indignation, Christ blasts the scribes and Pharisees one last time (Matthew 23).

Eight times Jesus pronounces "woe' upon the scribes and Pharisees. "Woe" is a word of solemn denunciation of punishment; it implies that great calamities of the most awful nature are impending over the guilty from the divine justice. Christ calls them hypocrites seven times. He refers to them as blind guides, fools and blind, whited sepulchres, serpents, and a generation of vipers. Two piercing thoughts are "How can ye escape the damnation of hell?" and "Behold, your house is left unto you desolate." Take a moment to read the entire chapter.

Conclusion

Have you seen Jesus? Does this chapter change your thinking a little? This is a side we sometimes do not want to see. Make no mistake, our Lord could be angered.

If we compiled a list of things that stirred up the anger of Christ it would include these:

1. Not being prepared when ample opportunity has been given.
2. Unbelief in the face of indisputable testimony.
3. Lack of looking on the inward man.
4. Thinking in physical terms and not spiritual.
5. Lack of understanding of the concept of grace.

Sadly these five things are present in the lives of many today. Undoubtedly the anger of Christ is kindled in heaven afar as He sees those on earth making the same mistakes of generations before them.

We should also note that Christ's anger was rarely, if ever, kindled against an alien sinner who knew nothing of God. It was always toward those who considered themselves religious and had the opportunity to learn about God and His will for man.

Lesson #6

Locate Where They Are Found

1. "Ye blind guide, which strains at a gnat, and swallow a camel." ________
2. "The blood of all the prophets, which was shed from the foundation of the world, may be required of this generation." ________
3. "O generation of vipers, how can ye, being evil, speak good things?" ________
4. "But I know you, that ye have not the love of God in you." ________
5. "They bind heavy burdens. . . but they themselves will not move them with one of their fingers." ________
6. "Ye are of your father the devil, and the lusts of your father ye will do." ________
7. "Full well ye reject the commandments of God, that ye may keep your own tradition." ________
8. "It shall be more tolerable for Tyre and Sidon at the day of judgment, than for you." ________
9. "Have ye your heart yet hardened?" ________
10. But when Jesus saw it, he was much displeased. ________

Thought Questions

1. What are five things that stirred up the anger of Christ?
   a. ________
   b. ________
   c. ________
   d. ________
   e. ________
2. Can you add more? ________
3. Apply those five things to people today. Are there those that fall into each category? Give examples. ________
4. Is Christ's attitude toward them today any different than it was toward those we studied in today's lesson? ________
5. Is this a seldom studied side of Christ? Why? ________

Chapter 7

LIVING IN THE WORLD

One thing that is of great concern to every Christian is, what is our attitude to be toward the world? How are we to deal with those who have a worldly nature? We know that evil companions corrupt good morals. We understand that we are called out of the world. But at the same time, we, who have our face set for heaven, must live out our time in our earthly tabernacle. Again, we don't want to express an attitude by our actions that makes others think we feel "too good" to have dealings with them.

Let's make this thought a little more personal. How should I treat my neighbor who has regular beer parties? What should be my attitude toward my co-workers who constantly tell vulgar jokes? How should I act toward individuals that I know are living a sexually immoral life?

As we have done throughout this study, let's take a closer look at the life of Jesus with special attention to the above kinds of situations. What was Jesus' attitude toward the world? What did He have to say concerning how we should relate to those who have a worldly nature?

Matthew

"And he went forth again by the sea side; and all the multitude resorted unto him, and he taught them. And as he passed by, he saw Levi the son of Alphaeus sitting at the receipt of custom, and said unto him, 'Follow me.' And he arose and followed him. And it came to pass, that, as Jesus sat at meat in his house, many publicans and sinners sat also together with Jesus and his disciples: for there were many, and they followed him. And when the scribes and Pharisees saw him eat with publicans and sinners, they said unto his disciples, 'How is it that he eateth and drinketh with publicans and sinners?' When Jesus heard it, he saith unto them, 'They that are whole have no need of a physician, but they that are sick: I came not to call the righteous but sinners to repentance.' " (Mark 2:13-17). From the parallel accounts in Matthew 9 and Luke 5 we learn that Levi and Matthew are the same individual.

Because another point in this lesson centers on a publican, or tax collector, it is important that the reader have a good understanding of their character in general and the attitude of the populace toward them. "In Judea, under the Roman system, all circumstances combined to make the publican the object of bitter hatred. He represented and exercised in immediate contact, at a sore spot with individuals, the hated power of Rome. The tax itself was looked upon as an inherent religious wrong, as well as civil imposition, and by many the payment of it was considered a sinful act of disloyalty to God. The tax gatherer, if a Jew, was a renegade in the eyes of his patriotic fellows. He paid a fixed sum for the taxes, and received for himself what he could over and above that amount. The ancient and widespread curse of arbitrariness was in the system. The collector was always under the suspicion of being an extortioner and probably *was* in most instances. The usual combination in a publican of petty tyrant, renegade and extortioner, made by circumstances almost inevitable, was not conducive to popularity." (*The International Standard Bible Encyclopedia,* Vol. 5, p. 2920).

Matthew was in the situation of being doubly hated because he was both a tax collector and Jew. Regarded as a traitor of his people he was treated as an outcast by them. A lonely and desperate man, Matthew was forced to find friends and fellowship among his fellow publicans and among the sinners who had little or no regard for God.

How does Jesus treat this outcast of Jewish society? He challenges him to take up the most noble cause in the world. "Follow me." Jesus gives Matthew the greatest honor that could be bestowed upon mortal man, a personal invitation from the lips of the son of God to take up his cross and follow Him.

Jesus went so far as to actually go to this man's home and eat a meal with him and his friends. And remember what kind of friends Matthew was forced to have. This is why the scribes and Pharisees were so appalled.

Why did Jesus reach out to this man and his friends? "They that are whole have no need of the physician, but they that are sick." These people needed the Great Physician the most.

What can we learn from this incident? Jesus saw not only what Matthew *was*, but more importantly what he *could be*. Too often we see someone involved in sin and decide they would not be helpful to the cause of Christ and we don't make the effort to reach out to them. While it is true that sinners are not helpful to the cause of Christ, let's always remember that sinners are what the cause of Christ is all about. We must look past the actions and see the value of their soul and see the good they can accomplish with Christ in their life. All souls are important to God.

Christ issued an invitation to Matthew to "follow me." But to demonstrate to Matthew that the invitation was not given just to be polite or just to make Himself look compassionate in front of the crowd, Jesus went to his house with him. It's one thing to knock on the door of someone and invite them to worship with us, but it is quite another thing to go into that person's home and sit down and take the time to show them that we are truly concerned for their welfare.

Jesus was so concerned about Matthew and so determined to do what was right that He did not let the fear of what others would think stop Him. Sometimes we are reluctant to be seen with those who have a bad reputation about town for fear of what others might say about us. We hesitate for fear of being ridiculed and made fun of. May we have the resolve of Jesus and be more concerned with calling sinners to repentance than being constantly in the company of the righteous.

Luke 15

In Luke 15 Christ tells three parables to the Pharisees to try and help them understand why He welcomed, ate with, and taught sinners. Whereas the Pharisees thought that those who were lost were not worthy of their effort to try and save, Jesus uses three examples to show them they would put forth the effort for physical things that were lost, why not for men's souls?

The Lost Sheep

"What man of you, having an hundred sheep, if he lose one of them, doth not leave the ninety and nine in the wilderness, and go after that which is lost, until he find it? And when he hath found it, he layeth it on his shoulders, rejoicing. And when he cometh home, he calleth his friends and neighbors, saying unto them, 'Rejoice with me: for I have found my sheep which was lost.' I say unto you, that likewise joy shall be in heaven over one sinner that repenteth, more than over ninety and nine just persons, which need no repentance" (vs. 4-7).

Everyone listening to Christ's words concerning looking for a lost sheep would be shaking his head in agreement. Probably most in the audience had actually done the very thing Christ was describing, at sometime in their life. Christ makes the point that just as men are happy when they find a lost sheep, so God in heaven is made happy when a lost soul is saved.

The Lost Coin

"Either what woman having ten pieces of silver, if she lose one piece, doth not light a candle, and sweep the house, and seek diligently till she find it? And when she hath found it, she calleth her friends and her neighbors together, saying, 'Rejoice with me; for I have found the piece which I had lost.' Likewise, I say unto you, there is joy in the presence of the angels of God over one sinner that repenteth." (vs. 8-10).

Once again the scene Christ drew for these Pharisees was undoubtedly all too familiar. No amount of energy would be too great for them to expend in searching for a lost coin. And the same point is made by Christ regarding the parallel between their joy over finding a lost coin and God's joy at the salvation of a lost soul.

The Lost Son

"A certain man had two sons: and the younger of them said to his father, 'Father, give me the portion of goods that falleth to me.' And he divided unto them his living. And not many days after the younger son gathered all together, and took his journey into a far country, and there wasted his substance with riotous living. And when he had spent all, there arose a mighty famine in that land; and he began to be in want. And he went and joined himelf to a citizen of that country; and he sent him into his fields to feed swine. And he would fain have filled his belly with the husks that the swine did eat: and no man gave unto him. And when he came to himself, he said, 'How many hired servants of my father's have bread and to spare, and I perish with hunger! I will arise and go to my father, and will say unto him, "Father, I have sinned against heaven, and before thee, and am no more worthy to be called thy son: make me as one of thy hired servants." ' And he arose, and came to his father. But when he was yet a great way off, his father saw him, and had compassion, and ran, and fell on his neck, and kissed him. And the son said unto him, 'Father, I have sinned against heaven, and in thy sight, and am no more worthy to be called thy son.' But the father said to his servants, 'Bring forth the best robe, and put it on him; and put a ring on his hand, and shoes on his feet: and bring hither the fatted calf, and kill it; and let us eat and be merry: for this my son was dead, and is alive again; he was lost, and is found.' And they began to be merry" (vs. 11-24).

Although this story is not one everyone might have experienced, all could certainly empathize with the story. All the Pharisees, had they been the father in the story, would have felt the same way—heart sick over his son's leaving, worried about his safety during the period of time he was gone, and overjoyed at his return. Perhaps tears were welling in their eyes as Jesus told this story.

But Jesus, the master story teller, knowing that the Pharisees were identifying themselves with the father in the story, continues his story and portrays their true nature toward lost souls in the character of the elder brother.

"Now his elder son was in the field: and as he came and drew nigh to the house, he heard music and dancing. And he called one of the servants, and asked what these things meant. And he said unto him, 'Thy brother is come; and thy father hath killed the fatted calf, because he hath received him safe and sound.' And he was angry, and would not go in: therefore came his father out, and entreated him. And he answering said to his father, 'Lo, these many years do I serve thee, neither transgressed I at any time thy commandment: and yet thou never gavest me a kid, that I might make merry with my friends: but as soon as this thy son was come, which hath devoured thy living with harlots, thou hast killed for him the fatted calf.' And he said unto him, 'Son, thou art ever with me, and all I have is thine. It was meet that we should make merry, and be glad: for this thy brother was dead, and is alive again; and was lost, and is found' " (vs. 25-32).

What is Jesus saying in these three parables to you and me about living in the world? No person, no matter how sinful or evil, could be classified as "not worth the effort" to talk to them about salvation. In many ways we are like the Pharisees, in having more concern for lost physical things than for lost souls. We are a long way from comprehending just how much importance God places on the saving of just one soul. Not until we recognize this importance will we be eager to meet and associate with those in the world with the intention of teaching them.

Zacchaeus

"And Jesus entered and passed through Jericho. And, behold, there was a man named Zacchaeus, which was the chief among the publicans, and he was rich. And he sought to see Jesus who he was: and could not for the press, because he was little of stature. And he ran before and climbed up into a sycamore tree to see him: for he was to pass that way. And when Jesus came to the place, he looked up, and saw him, and said unto him, 'Zacchaeus, make haste, and come down; for today I must abide at thy house.' And he made haste, and came down, and received him joyfully. And when they saw it, they all murmured, saying, that he was gone to be guest with a man that is a sinner. And Zacchaeus stood, and said unto the Lord; 'Behold, Lord, the half of my goods I give to the poor; and if I have taken any thing from any man by false accusation, I restore him fourfold.' And Jesus said unto him, 'This day is salvation come to this house, forsomuch as he also is a son of Abraham. For the Son of man is come to seek and to save that which was lost.' " (Luke 19:1-10).

The importance of this scene in Christ's life is not that Zacchaeus was "a wee little man" or that he climbed a sycamore tree. The importance is that once again we see Jesus, to the consternation of the Jews, reach out to one who was considered a chief sinner. Jesus did not condemn Zacchaeus simply because of the group he belonged to (publicans). As in the case of Matthew, Jesus saw big potential in this small man.

Conclusion

From these lessons Jesus taught what can we conclude about what our attitude toward the world should be? First of all we must not let our aversion toward sin or our hatred of it prevent us from teaching those who are in sin.

Secondly, we should look more at what a person can become, with the power of God, than at what they are.

Thirdly, unless we show ourselves to be friendly, compassionate, interested people we will not be able to reach others. Most people are converted only after having developed a friendly relationship with a Christian.

Fourthly, we are to be friends with the world as long as it does not have more influence on us than we do on it. Remember, Christ could do many things we cannot. He was *always* stronger than *anyone* He associated with. We are not made that way. There will be those who can influence us for evil. These are the ones we *must avoid* until we can show ourselves stronger than they.

We, as Christians, are in the world to save the world. Our light cannot shine in the world unless we go to the world.

Lesson #7
Locate Where They Are Found

1. Then drew near unto him all the publicans and sinners to hear him. ____
____

2. "How is it that he eateth and drinketh with publicans and sinners?" ____
____

3. There was a man named Zacchaeus, which was the chief among the publicans. . . he sought to see Jesus. ____
____

4. "I say unto you, that likewise joy shall be in heaven over one sinner that repenteth, more than over ninety and nine just persons, which need no repentance." ____

5. And when they saw it, they all murmured, saying, that he was gone to be guest with a man that is a sinner. ____

6. "They that are whole have no need of the physician, but they that are sick." ____

7. "Likewise, I say unto you, there is joy is the presence of the angels of God over one sinner that repenteth." ____

8. "I came not to call the righteous, but sinners to repentance." ____
____

9. "For the Son of man is come to seek and to save that which was lost." ____
____

10. "But when he was yet a great way off, his father saw him." ____
____

Thought Questions

1. Who did Jesus come into the world to save? ____
____

2. Why are we sometimes hesitant to reach out to those who are living in the wallows of sin? ____
____

3. Does the fact that we are called out of the world mean we are to have nothing to do with the world? ____
____

4. What could Christ do that we cannot that should cause us to have caution in our dealings with the world? ______________________

____

5. How would you explain what our attitude should be towards the world? __

____

Chapter 8

COUNT THE COST

"I didn't know being a Christian was so hard."

"I didn't realize that following Christ meant so much."

"I thought once I became a Christian everything would be easy."

Statements like the ones above are heard many times by preachers and elders. People who make such statements have not seen Jesus clearly. They have misunderstood what is expected of His followers.

Christ never said it would be easy to follow Him. On the contrary, He states plainly many times that one must be willing to pay a heavy cost to take up the cross of Christ as a way of life. Perhaps we have not looked closely enough at this side of Jesus. Have we been guilty of teaching that "the Christian life is the easiest life in the world?" (Meaning one without problems, temptations, or difficulties.)

Once, when talking to His followers about the trials they must undergo, Christ said, "I have told you this, so that when the time comes you will remember that I warned you" (John 16:4 NIV). Maybe we need to look again at the cost of discipleship so that we might examine ourselves to see if we are willing to pay the price. As you read this chapter ask yourself at each of the points, "Have I paid this price?"

Mark 9:35-10:45 The Cost? Service, Severing Ties, Persecutions, and Sacrifices

Be a servant to all. "And he sat down, and called the twelve, and saith unto them, 'If any man desire to be first, the same shall be last of all, and servant of all.' " (Mark 9:35).

This statement by Christ is made in response to an argument the twelve had regarding who was the greatest. Of all the traits of Christ that the twelve tried to imitate, this one was perhaps one they had the greatest difficulty accepting. They wanted places of great prestige and glory in the kingdom. To be a servant to anyone went against their nature.

A servant is one whose sole task is to wait on another. His desire is to help and make life easier for someone else. He thinks of others before he thinks of himself. And notice that Christ does not tell them just to be servants to the other twelve. Serving those who are pleasant and agreeable requires little or no effort on our part. We are to be servant to *all.*

We must be willing to sever ourselves from anything that causes us to sin. "And if thy hand offend thee, cut it off: it is better for thee to enter into life maimed, than having two hands to go into hell, into the fire that never shall be quenched: where their worm dieth not, and the fire is not quenched. And if thy foot offend thee, cut it off: it is better for thee to enter halt into life, than having two feet to be cast into hell, into the fire that never shall be quenched: where their worm dieth not, and the fire is not quenched. And if thine eye offend thee, pluck it out: it is better for thee to enter into the kingdom of God with one eye, than having two eyes to be cast into hell fire: where their own worm dieth not, and the fire is not quenched'" (Mark 9:43-48).

Using as strong an example as the human mind could comprehend, Christ told the twelve if a part of their physical body caused them to sin it should be amputated. The true meaning of his statement is, of course, symbolical. There are often situations or people that we, as a result of our commitment to Christ, will have to separate or sever ourselves from. It might be friends who cause us to stumble. There always seems to be one or two people who can lead us to sin more than others. These are the ones we must sever ourselves from.

Sometimes it is family that we must sever ourselves from if they are keeping us from doing what is right. One of the most difficult steps a person has to make sometimes is to break away from the way his family has done things for generations. The pressure to not break the family tradition is tremendous. But when those traditions are keeping us from doing what Christ says, we must break away.

It might be an occupation that we must give up if it is causing us to sin. It could be that the nature of the business itself is sinful, making or distribution of alcoholic beverages, producing or selling pornographic material, or it might be that the people you work with, because of their influence, cause you to sin.

Part of the cost of discipleship might be the giving up of some social activities that entice us to commit sin.

Everyone will be "salted with fire." For every one shall be salted with fire, and every sacrifice shall be salted with salt" (Mark 9:49).

Salt, when mentioned in the Bible, has reference to preservation. And fire refers to trials and persecutions. Therefore Christ is telling us to expect trials and persecutions, such as severing ourselves from things that cause us to sin, in order that we might have the opportunity to show ourselves worthy of God's grace.

We must be willing to give up what we love most if it stands between us and God. "And when he was gone forth into the way, there came one running, and kneeled to him, and asked him, 'Good Master, what shall I do that I may inherit eternal life?' And Jesus said unto him, 'Why callest thou me good? there is none good but one, that is, God. Thou knowest the commandments, Do not commit adultery, Do not kill, Do not steal, Do not bear false witness, Defraud not, Honor thy father and mother.' And he answered and said unto him, 'Master, all these have I observed from my youth.' Then Jesus beholding him loved him, and said unto him, 'One thing thou lackest: go thy way, sell whatsoever thou hast, and give to the poor, and thou shalt have treasure in heaven: and come, take up the cross and follow me.' And he was sad at that saying, and went away grieved: for he had great possessions" (Mark 10:17-22).

This young man had done many great things in the keeping of the law. He did not commit adultery, didn't kill, didn't steal, etc. But he loved his money. Christ, knowing the hearts of men as He did, saw that this man loved his money more than God. Therefore the cost of discipleship for this individual was to give his fortune away.

The cost of discipleship will be different for each of us because our love of worldly things differs. But whatever we love more than God, that is what must be given up.

With blessings come persecutions. "Verily I say unto you, There is no man that hath left house, or brethren, or sisters, or father, or mother, or wife, or children, or lands, for my sake, and the gospel's, but he shall receive an hundredfold now in this time, houses, and brethren, and sisters, and mothers, and children, and lands, with persecutions; and in the world to come eternal life" (Mark 10:29-30).

Notice the great blessing Christ promised to those who sacrificed in order to follow Him. Note also that He did not paint an all rosy picture but assured them of persecutions. Just as sure as we will be blessed for following Christ we will be persecuted, also.

Drink the bitter cup of persecution and be baptized with overwhelming suffering. "Ye know not what ye ask: can ye drink of the cup that I drink of? and be baptized with the baptism that I am baptized with?" And they said unto him, "We can." And Jesus said unto them, "Ye shall indeed drink of the cup that I drink of; and with the baptism that I am baptized withal shall ye be baptized" (Mark 10:38-39).

The cup Jesus drank of was the cup of persecution. The baptism He referred to was the baptism of suffering, overwhelming in nature. Part of the cost of discipleship is sharing with Christ in these things.

Become a servant and slave to all. "But so shall it not be among you: but whosoever will be great among you, shall be your minister: and whosoever of you will be of the chiefest, shall be servant of all" (Mark 10:43-44).

The cross of Christ is a cross of service. If we are to take up that cross we must be willing to lay pride aside and offer ourselves to minister to others.

John 6 The Cost?
Belief, Accepting Christ As A Way Of Life

Believe on Christ. "This is the work of God, that ye believe on him whom he hath sent. And this is the will of him that sent me, that every one which seeth the Son, and believeth on him, may have everlasting life: and I will raise him up the last day. Verily, verily, I say unto you, he that believeth on me hath everlasting life." (vs. 29,40,47).

Eat Christ's flesh and drink his blood. "I am the living bread which came down from heaven: if any man eat of this bread, he shall live forever: and the bread that I will give is my flesh, which I will give for the life of the world." The Jews therefore strove among themselves, saying, "How can this man give us his flesh to eat? Then Jesus said unto them, "Verily, verily, I say unto you, except ye eat the flesh of the Son of man, and drink his blood, ye have no life in you. Whoso eateth my flesh, and drinketh my blood, hath eternal life; and I will raise him up at the last day. For my flesh is meat indeed, and my blood is drink indeed. He that eateth my flesh, and drinketh my blood, dwelleth in me, and I in him. As the living Father hath sent me, and I live by the Father: so he that eateth me, even he shall live by me. This is that bread which came down from heaven: not as your fathers did eat manna, and are dead: he that eateth of this bread shall live for ever." (vs. 51-58).

Christ tells this audience that they must eat His flesh and drink His blood. This means that a person must take on the nature of Christ. Just as the Father's will became Christ's will, so Christ's will is to become our will. Christ's life is to become our life. We become more and more like Him and thereby take on His nature.

Luke 14:25-35 The Cost? Family, Life, Carry Own Cross, Total Commitment

Love Christ more than family. "If any man come to me, and hate not his father, and mother, and wife, and children, and brethren, and sisters, yea and his own life also, he cannot be my disciple" (vs. 26).

Some of the strongest attachments and feelings we have are for members of our family. But our love for Christ must be greater. We must not let our family keep us from doing God's will.

Love Christ over own life. "If any man come to me and hate not his own life he cannot be my disciple" (vs. 26).

We live in an age of personal gratification. Whatever we want, we get. "I owe it to myself. . . " "I want to do *my* own thing." "I have *my* rights." "It's *my* life. I can do what *I* want to."

Christ says we have to give up living for self. *Our* will doesn't matter any more. We must sacrifice personal pleasure for the sake of carrying the cross of Christ.

Carry our own cross. "And whosoever doth not bear his cross, and come after me, cannot be my disciple" (v. 27).

Everyone will have to sacrifice something in order to follow Christ. For some it will be family, for others personal pleasure, for others various things. This is each person's cross or burden to bear. This is the price we have to pay. We must be willing to bear it.

Give up everything. "So likewise, whosoever he be of you that forsaketh not all that he hath, he cannot be my disciple" (v. 33).

This statement by Christ is the application of the two parables told in vs. 28-32 concerning the importance of considering the cost before getting involved in any venture in life. More importantly, we must not enter rashly into the Christian life. We must weigh seriously the cost. When the cost is totaled up it amounts to a willingness to give up everything in order to be a disciple of Christ.

John 14-16 The Cost? Follow Christ's Footsteps, Obedience, Bear Fruit, Suffer Persecution and Trials

The conversation found in the 14th through 16th chapters of the book of John is a very personal talk from Jesus to His disciples. It takes place Thursday night before Christ's arrest.

Must follow Christ's footsteps, even do greater things. "Verily, verily, I say unto you, he that believeth on me, the works that I do shall he do also; and greater works than these shall he do; because I go unto my Father" (14:12).

We must study closely the life of Christ and the things He did and pattern our lives accordingly. And in a remarkable statement Christ says that His followers would do even *greater* works. The apostles proved Him true by converting more in one day (3,000 on Pentecost) than Christ had converted during His earthly ministry.

Our opportunities in the 20th century are even greater. Think of all the conveniences we have that enable us to reach even more people—radio, television, mass mailings, transportation. We must use these opportunities!

"If ye love me, keep my commandments" (14:15). This is the divine test of love. The amount of love we have for Christ is directly proportionate to the amount of desire we have to do His will. A person's love for Christ can be measured by his obedience to His will and vice-versa. One is never greater than the other; they go hand in hand. (also note 14:23; 15:10,14.)

Bear fruit. "I am the true vine, and my Father is the husbandman. Every branch in me that beareth not fruit he taketh away" (15:1-2).

Christ makes it plain here that bearing fruits is not an option, it is a requirement. It is one of the marks of a disciple. Punishment is a certainty for those who do not bear fruit.

Be pruned. "Every branch that beareth fruit, he purgeth it, that it may bring forth more fruit" (15:2).

Using the figure of the grape vine, Christ says that fruit bearing branches are "purged" or "trimmed" (NIV) in order to make them more fruitful. This is a scientific principle long recognized by fruit growers. Pruning a plant makes it more productive.

The prunings we must undergo are trials, temptations, persecutions, etc. Notice this is promised not to unfruitful but to fruitful servants. True disciples will respond to this with renewed effort to bear fruit.

Be hated by the world. "If the world hate you, ye know that it hated me before it hated you. If ye were of the world, the world would love his own: but because ye are not of the world, but I have chosen you out of the world, therefore the world hateth you. Remember the word that I said unto you, The servant is not greater than his lord. If they have persecuted me, they will also persecute you" (15:18-20).

Yes, there will be times that we are hated by the world. Why? Because we are not of this world. We are of Christ and we are obedient to Him.

And because we bear fruit for Him. We need not be surprised when we are despised and rejected, for so was our Saviour before us.

Conclusion

Christ pulled no punches when telling others of the cost of discipleship. He made no attempt to paint an all rosy picture of what the life of a Christian would be like. While the pathways of heaven may be paved with gold, the pathway of discipleship is not. The cost is high: service, severing ties, persecutions, sacrifice, belief, accepting Christ as a way of life, family, life, carry own cross, total commitment, follow Christ's footsteps, obedience, bear fruit, suffer persecutions and trials.

We who are children of God must ask ourselves: "Have I really paid the price of discipleship?"

Lesson #8
Locate Where They Are Found

1. "If any man desire to be first, the same shall be last of all, and servant of all." ____________________
2. "If the world hate you, ye know that it hated me before it hated you." ____________________
3. "So likewise, whosoever he be of you that forsaketh not all that he hath, he cannot be my disciple." ____________________
4. "If ye love me, keep my commandments." ____________________
5. "And if thy hand offend thee, cut if off." ____________________
6. "This is the work of God, that ye believe on him whom he hath sent." ____________________
7. "If any man come to me, and hate not his father, and mother, and wife, and children, and brethren, and sisters, yea, and his own life also, he cannot be my disciple." ____________________
8. "Herein is my Father glorified, that ye bear much fruit; so shall ye be my disciples." ____________________
9. "Whoso eateth my flesh, and drinketh my blood, hath eternal life." ____________________
10. "But whosoever will be great among you, shall be your minister." ____________________

Thought Questions

1. Why is the cost of discipleship sometimes different for different people? ___

   ____.

2. List fifteen items given at the conclusion of the lesson that constitute the cost of discipleship. As you list each one ask yourself, "Have I really paid the cost?

   1. ______________________________
   2. ______________________________
   3. ______________________________
   4. ______________________________
   5. ______________________________
   6. ______________________________
   7. ______________________________
   8. ______________________________
   9. ______________________________
   10. ______________________________
   11. ______________________________
   12. ______________________________
   13. ______________________________
   14. ______________________________
   15. ______________________________

3. How would you respond to someone who said, "the cost of following Christ is too great?" ______________________________

   ____

4. Could you use this lesson to teach the falsehood of salvation by "faith only?" ______________________________

   ____

5. Why do you think Christ emphasized so strongly the cost of discipleship?

   ____

Chapter 9

WHAT ARE YOU DOING FOR CHRIST?

On the Judgement Day when we stand before the throne of justice many of us will undoubtedly be condemned when we answer the Judge's question, "What did you do for me while you were living on earth?" One of the most important questions one can ever ask himself is, what am I doing for Christ?

Everything a Christian does is for Christ whether it is a positive way or a negative way. What many of us wonder is, is what I am doing pleasing Christ? am I doing enough? how much is enough? what does Jesus expect of me as a child of His?

In this chapter we will try to answer these questions by looking at four incidents or scenes from Christ's life.

Simon the Pharisee And the Sinful Woman

"And one of the Pharisee's desired him that he would eat with him, And he went into the Pharisees's house, and sat down to meat. And, behold, a woman in the city, which was a sinner, when she knew that Jesus sat at meat in the Pharisees's house, brought an alabaster box of ointment, and stood at his feet behind him weeping,and began to wash his feet with tears, and did wipe them with the hairs of her head, and kissed his feet, and anointed them with the ointment. Now when the Pharisee which had bidden him saw it, he spake within himself, saying, 'This man, if he were a prophet, would have known who and what manner of woman this is that toucheth him: for she is a sinner.' And Jesus answering said unto him, 'Simon, I have somewhat to say unto thee.' And he saith, 'Master, say on.' There was a certain creditor which had two debtors: the one owed five hundred pence, and the other fifty. And when they had nothing to pay, he frankly forgave them both. Tell me therefore, which of them will love him most?' Simon answered and said, 'I suppose that he, to whom he forgave most.' And he turned to the woman, and said unto Simon, 'Seest thou this woman? I entered into thine house, thou gavest me no water for my feet: but she hath washed my feet with tears, and wiped them with the hairs of her head. Thou gavest me no kiss: but this woman since the time I came in hath not ceased to kiss my feet. My head with oil thou didst not anoint: but this woman hath anointed my feet with ointment. Wherefore I say unto thee, her sins, which are many, are forgiven; for she loved much: but to whom little is forgiven, the same loveth little.' And he said unto her, 'Thy sins are forgiven' " (Luke 7:36-48).

Let's look at Simon and this woman and notice what each had done for Christ. It is important for us to determine which one was pleasing Jesus and why their actions were pleasing to Him.

Simon the Pharisee had asked Jesus to come home and eat a meal with him. He probably thought he had done a great thing in having this celebrity named Jesus into his home. He might have hoped it would cause quite a stir in social circles. But Simon gave no special treatment for his guest. He really made no special arrangements since he was going to have a meal anyway. His having Jesus into his home did not break his normal routine. What he had done for Jesus was what was easy and convenient for him.

It would be hard to paint a picture more beautiful than the description of what the sinful woman did for Christ. Notice closely: she stood behind Him; she washed His feet with her tears; she then wiped them with her hair; then she kissed His feet; and finally anointed then with fragrant oil. In so doing this woman demonstrated her faith in Christ just by her presence in a hostile crowd. We see her repentance in the tears she shed. The depth of her love was made manifest by her using her hair. The deep love this woman had for Jesus she demonstrated by kissing His feet. And her willingness to sacrifice for Him is seen in the use of the costly ointment. Each of us should be deeply humbled and ashamed in the presence of this woman.

Simon the Pharisee did for Jesus what was easy and convenient. He served expecting great things and received nothing. The sinful woman did for Jesus what others thought too lowly to do. She did beyond measure. She served expecting nothing and received everything.

Who are we most like, Simon or the woman?

The Rich Young Ruler

"And behold, one came and said unto him, 'Good Master, what good thing shall I do, that I may have eternal life?' And he said unto him, 'Why callest me good? there is none good but one, that is, God: but if thou wilt enter into life, keep the commandments.' He said unto him, 'Which?' Jesus said, 'Thou shalt do no murder, Thou shalt not commit adultery, Thou shalt not steal, Thou shalt not bear false witness, honour thy father and thy mother: and, thou shalt love thy neighbor as thyself.' The young man saith unto him, 'All these things have I kept from my youth up: what lack I yet?' Jesus said unto him, 'If thou wilt be perfect, go and sell that thou hast, and give to the poor, and thou shalt have treasure in heaven: come and follow me.' But when the young man heard that saying, he went away sorrowful: for he had great possessions" (Matthew 19:16-22).

It would seem at first that this rich young ruler would be one who would be acceptable to Christ. He had kept the commandments. He didn't murder, commit adultery, steal, or bear false witness. He honored his father and mother and loved his neighbor. He was serving God. So what was wrong?

Jesus saw immediately that this young man had done only those things he wanted to do not the things he needed to do. Thus Jesus challenges him to sell his possessions and give them to the poor. Doing only those things we want to do is not enough to satisfy Christ.

Are we like this young man?

Servants and Masters

"And the apostles said unto the Lord, 'Increase our faith.' And the Lord said, 'If ye had faith as a grain of mustard seed, ye might say unto this sycamore tree, be thou plucked up by the root, and be thou planted in the sea; and it should obey you. But which of you, having a servant plowing or feeding cattle, will say unto him by and by, when he is come from the field, "Go and sit down to meat?" And will not rather say unto him, "Make ready wherewith I may sup, and gird thyself, and serve me, till I have eaten and drunken; and afterward thou shalt eat and drink?" Doth he thank that servant because he did the things that were commanded him? I think not. So likewise ye, when ye shall have done all those things which are commanded you, say, we are unprofitable servants: we have done that which was our duty to do' " (Luke 17:5-10).

This is an often overlooked parable, perhaps due to the fact that we don't understand the servant-master relationship of that day. It first appears to be a harsh attitude on the part of the master for not having the servant come to eat after working in the field. And beyond that of having the servant prepare the meal for his master before he is allowed to eat himself. And more than that of having the servant serve the meal. But a servant in Christ's time would not think this a harsh attitude at all. And just as the master in the parable offers no thanks to the servant for what he has done, a servant of that day would not expect thanks for doing what was expected of him.

The application Christ makes is now easier to see. "So likewise ye, when he shall have done all those things which are commanded you, say, we are unprofitable servants: we have done that which was our duty to do." We are servants in the Kingdom. Christ is our master. When we think we have done so much for Christ that we deserve a break, or the praise of others, we need to say we are unprofitable servants because we have only done what was our duty to do.

The Widow's Mite

"And Jesus sat over against the treasury, and beheld how the people cast money into the treasury: and many that were rich cast in much. And there came a certain poor widow, and she threw in two mites, which make a farthing. And he called unto him his disciples, and saith unto them, 'Verily I say unto you, that this poor widow hath cast more in, than all they which have cast into the treasury: for all they did cast in of their abundance; but she of her want did cast in all that she had, even all her living' " (Mark 12:41-44).

Jesus, the great observer of human nature, uses the example of the widow to teach His disciples a very important lesson concerning serving God. Again we have a great contrast in this story. Some giving great amounts of money and the widow giving two mites. Christ offers not one word of praise to those who had given the great amounts but focuses His praise on the widow. Why?

The amount we give or do for God is not what's important. Those who had given the large amounts of money had done no great thing for God because they had done what was easy, simple, and convenient for them. "They did cast in of their abundance." But the widow had done what was difficult and sacrificial in giving her two mites. She gave all she had. "She of her want did cast in all that she had, even all her living."

No doubt the rich men were very pompous in their parading before the treasury with their gifts. They thought they were doing much and would receive the praise of others. But Christ shows them to have done little.

The widow probably approached the treasury humbly and perhaps even a little embarrassed as she saw how meager her offering looked when compared to the ones given before her. She thought she was doing little when in fact she did more than all the rich before her put together.

Conclusion

Having looked at these four scenes from the life of Christ, we must return to the original question, what are you doing for Christ?

When it comes to worshipping Christ do you assemble with the saints only when you feel like it? when the weather is nice? when you don't have any other plans? In other words, only when it is convenient for you and you don't have to go to any trouble?

When it comes to giving of your means to the cause of Christ, which character in this chapter are you like? Remember the amount is not what is important to Christ, it is how much you are willing to sacrifice. We must give more than is easy for us to give. Our giving must be of a sacrificial nature.

What about when it comes to showing concern for the lost? Do you consent to "knock doors" only when you can't find anything else better to do? Do you look for opportunities to reach out to others or do you let opportunities come looking for you?

When do you let your Christian light shine? only when it is easy? only when it does not cost you anything? only when you don't have to sacrifice some personal pleasure? only when you want to?

When we reach the point in our Christian lives that we think we should be proud of our accomplishments, that we deserve the praise of God and others, when we think we have done enough, we need to remember Christ's words, "So, likewise ye, when shall have done all those things which are commanded you, say, we are unprofitable servants: we have done that which was our duty to do."

Lesson #9

Locate Where They Are Found

1. "If thou wilt enter into life, keep the commandments." ______________

____

2. And the apostles said unto the Lord, "Increase our faith."

____

3. And there came a certain poor widow, and she threw in two mites. ______

____

4. And, behold, a woman in the city, which was a sinner. . . and stood at his feet behind him weeping, and began to wash his feet with tears. ________

____

5. But when the young man heard that saying, he went away sorrowful: for he had great possessions. ______________________________

6. "She of her want did cast in all that she had." ________________

____

7. "When ye shall have done all those things which are commanded you, say, We are unprofitable servants: we have done that which was our duty to do." ______________________________

8. "My head with oil thou didst not anoint: but this woman hath anointed my feet with ointment." ______________________________

9. "Verily I say unto you, that this poor widow hath cast more in, than all they which have cast into the treasury." ____________________

10. "Doth he thank that servant because he did the things that were commanded him?" ______________________________

Thought Questions

1. Why did Jesus praise the sinful woman in Luke 7:36-50 and not Simon the Pharisee? ______________________________

____

2. Why didn't Jesus praise the rich young ruler for keeping the commandments of the law? ______________________________

____

3. What is the lesson for us to learn from the parable in Luke 17:5-10? ____

____

4. How do you keep a lesson like the one we've just studied from making you feel like there's no use in trying to live a Christian life because I'll never do all I'm capable of doing? ______________________________

____

5. Can you know when you've done enough for Christ? If so, how? ________

____

Chapter 10

TOUCHING PEOPLE WHERE THEY HURT

Suppose a farmer decides he wants to plant some corn. After making this decision, he goes to a field that has never been under cultivation but is covered in pasture. He then takes a sack of seed corn and starts sowing it by hand and goes home to wait for the seed to produce. We would say that farmer is foolish, wouldn't we? Much preparation has to be made to soil before it is ready to receive the seed into its womb and produce a plant.

This is the same principle we find Jesus teaching in the parable of the soils (Matthew 13). Christ, the master teacher, knew the importance of this fact as it related to sowing the words of life in the hearts of man. A man's heart must be opened and softened before the seed of the kingdom can reach its fullest potential. This is why we see Jesus time and time again touching people's lives where they hurt the most. He knew that until the hurt was removed they would not be able to think on spiritual things.

In this chapter we will note three instances where Christ used this principle to achieve great success.

The Nobleman's Son

"So Jesus came again into Cana of Galilee, where he made the water wine. And there was a certain nobleman, whose son was sick at Capernaum. When he heard that Jesus was come out to Judea into Galilee, he went unto him, and besought him that he would come down, and heal his son: for he was at the point of death. Then said Jesus unto him, 'Except ye see signs and wonders, ye will not believe.' The nobleman saith unto him, 'Sir, come down ere my child die.' Jesus saith unto him 'Go thy way; thy son liveth.' And the man believed the word that Jesus had spoken unto him, and he went his way. And as he was going down, his servants met him, and told him, saying, 'Thy son liveth.' Then inquired he of them the hour when he began to amend. And they said unto him, 'Yesterday at the seventh hour the fever left him.' So the father knew that it was at the same hour, in the which Jesus said unto him, 'Thy son liveth:' and himself believed, and his whole house" (John 4:46-53).

The situation here involves two important elements. One, the nobleman's son is at the point of death. Two, the nobleman and his family were nonbelievers.

What was Christ's response to this situation? He did not seize this as an opportunity to teach the nobleman the way of God. He did not demand an audience with the nobleman's household before He would heal his son. What He did do was heal the nobleman's son. Christ knew that the most important thing in that man's life at the immediate moment was to care for his son. He also knew that until this hurt was removed he would not be ready to listen to a message from God.

What was the nobleman's response to Christ's response? The Bible says that not only did he believe but, no doubt due to his words of testimony, his whole household also believed on Christ. The nobleman responded to a man who had touched him where he had hurt the most. He knew that here was a man who really cared about helping him.

The Crowd At Capernaum

"And they went into Capernaum. . . And there was in their synagogue a man with an unclean spirit. . . And Jesus rebuked him, saying, 'Hold thy peace, and come out of him.' And when the unclean spirit had torn him, and cried with a loud voice, he came out of him. . . And immediately his fame spread abroad throughout all the region round about Galilee. . . And at even, when the sun did set, they brought unto him all that were diseased, and them that were possessed with devils. And all the city was gathered together at the door. And he healed many that were sick of divers diseases, and cast out many devils; and suffered not the devils to speak, because they knew him. And Simon and they that were with him, they said unto him, 'All men seek for thee.' And he said unto them, 'Let us go into the next towns, that I may preach there also: for therefore came I forth' " (Mark 1:21-38).

Picture in your mind's eye for a moment the scene in the streets of Capernaum described in verses 32 and 33. As the sun sets on the city, the street where Jesus is staying swells with a vast multitude of diseased people. What a pitiful sight it must have been! The lame hobbling on make-shift crutches. Others carried in the arms of friends and loved ones. Some on stretchers. The blind haltingly proceeding to the house where release from their disease was hoped to be found.

What was Christ's response to this vast crowd? Once again, no sermon was given, no lecture delivered, no rebukes extended. Jesus healed them all.

What was the crowd's response to Christ's response? "And again he entered into Capernaum, after some days; and it was noised that he was in the house. And straightway many were gathered together, insomuch that there was no room to receive them, no, not so much as about the door: and he preached the word unto them" (Mark 2:1-2). The people literally mobbed him to hear the words He had to speak.

It is on this occasion that Christ healed the palsied man who was let down through the roof by his four friends. After seeing this demonstration of His caring for people the crowd sought after Him even more. "And he (Christ) went forth again by the sea side; and all the multitude resorted unto him, and he taught them" (Mark 2:13). The multitude eagerly gathered on the seashore to hear the wonderful words of life.

Why did the people respond to Christ in such a positive way? He had touched them where they hurt the most. They realized His first concern was in helping them.

The Crowd From Galilee

"But Jesus withdrew himself with his disciples to the sea: and a great multitude from Galilee followed him, and from Judaea, and from Jerusalem, and from Idumaea, and from beyond Jordan; and they about Tyre and Sidon, a great multitude, when they had heard what great things he did, came unto him. And he spake to his disciples that a small ship should wait on him because of the multitude, lest they should throng him. For he had healed many; insomuch that they pressed upon him for to touch him, as many as had plagues. And unclean spirits, when they saw him, fell down before him, and cried, saying, 'Thou art the Son of God.' And he straitly charged them that they should not make him known" (Mark 3:7-12).

Note the situation here. People from every region and town for miles around gathered to see and hear this Jesus. Perhaps it was an innumerable crowd. The number was so great and their enthusiasm to be close to Him so strong that there was concern on the part of Jesus for His own safety.

What caused such a multitude to assemble? "For he had healed many." He had been touching people where they hurt. Perhaps everyone in the crowd had been touched in some way by Jesus. Some He had healed earlier. Others may have had a loved one or friend that had been touched by the healing power of the Master's hand.

How did Christ respond to this situation? Through a chronological study of the New Testament, we learn that it was after this incident that Jesus delivered the Sermon on the Mount (Matthew 5-7). Jesus, having cured the people of their physical ills, tells them in that sermon the cure for their spiritual ills. The result of His teaching is recorded in Matthew 7:28. "The people were astonished at his doctrine."

Christ Knew Where To Sow The Seed

As noted in the introduction to this chapter, a farmer would be foolish to try and plant in rocky soil or thorny soil or no soil at all. Soil must be prepared to receive the seed. As seen in this chapter, Christ cultivated, or prepared, the people's hearts by helping them. He caused their hearts to be open, eager, and receptive even before He taught them. Thus the seed fell on fertile hearts that would produce a bountiful harvest.

What About Us Today?

We as members of the body of Christ are long overdue for some serious soul-searching questions. Are we *really* looking to help people? to touch them where they are hurting?

Let me relate a true experience to help us see this point more clearly. During one winter some small children in our community were noticed by their school teachers as never wearing a coat, no matter how cold the temperature. It also came to be known that they never wore undergarments. One of the local civic clubs investigated and found this family living in one room of a large country house. The only heat was from wood and paper burned in a fifty gallon drum that sat in the middle of the floor. They had only one change of clothes and no coats.

Immediately this civic club moved in to relieve this family by purchasing clothes, a wood stove, and food.

My first response when I heard about this incident was pride in this civic club. I was thrilled that there were people like them looking to help others. But on further reflection I thought, where was the church? With four hundred members scattered all across the area why didn't we see this family? I wondered how many more families there were in similar situations?

Conclusion

Reaching out and touching others where they hurt is not an easy task. It takes ever searching eyes, constantly looking for those who are hurting and for opportunities to help them. It takes hands willing to get dirty. Telling a hungry, cold man to go his way and be warmed and filled will not help that man. It is much easier to talk about those who need our help than it is to go out and actually help them. It takes knees willing to bend. Sometimes we let our pride in our social status keep us from going among those of low estate. We fear what others might say about us if they see us among the poor and lowly. But Christ went out of His way to condescend to those of low estate and so must we. It also takes a heart overflowing with love for mankind. A heart like this will have the ever searching eyes, the willing hands, and the bending knee.

Please don't misunderstand the message of this chapter. I am not preaching a social gospel. We are not to be limited in our efforts to just fill empty stomachs and binding up wounds. But Christ knew the value of helping others and we would profit by following His example.

Finally, let me share some thoughts taken from an article I read recently, "We're busy people—all of us. This is a fast paced society in which we live. We run on well-defined tracks. Little time to venture off our tracks and slow our pace to interact with people who are not imperative for our ongoing well being.

"But let's remember—we can and must continually extend the healing ministering hands of Christ because there are people hurting, families shattering, lives tormented, just two doors down." (from an article entitled "Two Doors Down" by John Scott.)

Lesson #10
Locate Where They Are Found

1. So the father knew that it was at the same hour, in the which Jesus said unto him, "Thy son liveth:" and himself believed, and his whole house. ____

   ____

2. Jesus saith unto him, "Go thy way; thy son liveth." ________________

   ____

3. "But he that receiveth seed into the good ground is he that heareth the word, and understandeth it; which also beareth fruit, and bringeth forth, some an hundredfold, some sixty, some thirty." ______________________

____

4. And he went forth again by the sea side; and all the multitude resorted unto him, and he taught them. ______________________

5. And it came to pass, when Jesus had ended these sayings, the people were astonished at his doctrine. ______________________

6. And at even, when the sun did set, they brought unto him all that were diseased, and them that were possessed with devils. ______________

____

7. "Behold a sower went forth to sow." ______________________

8. A great multitude, when they heard what great things he did, came unto him. ______________________

9. And all the city was gathered together at the door. ______________

____

10. For he had healed many; insomuch that they pressed upon him for to touch him, as many as had plagues. ______________________

Thought Questions

1. What does it mean to "touch people where they hurt?" ______________

____

2. What are some ways or areas in which people today are hurting? ________

____

3. What are some specific ways we can improve in this area? ____________

____

4. What does the "Parable of the Sower" have to do with this lesson? ______

____

5. Write down the name of one person you know who is hurting that you are going to help this week. ______________________

Chapter 11

THOSE WHO *DID* SEE JESUS

We began this study with a question, have you seen Jesus? The premise being that many in Christ's day thought they saw Him but did not and how many of us today have made the same error. In chapter one we focused on those who did not see Jesus. But not everyone was blind to Christ's nature and His mission. Some did see Him and understood who He was. This chapter will take a look at those individuals.

Simeon

Simeon was a just, devout man who was prayerfully waiting for the coming of the prophecied Messiah. When the time came for Joseph and Mary to present their child before the Lord in Jerusalem, the Holy Spirit operated directly on Simeon to reveal to him that Mary's child was the Messiah. Through his study of the Law he understood that Christ would be a man's means of salvation. "For mine eyes have seen thy salvation, which thou has prepared before the face of all people." (cf. Isaiah 52:10).

He also understood that Christ would be not only the saviour of the Jews but also of the Gentiles. "A light to lighten the Gentiles, and the glory of thy people Israel" (Isaiah 42:6).

And he knew that Christ would suffer and die, causing grief to His mother, Mary. "Yea, a sword shall pierce through thine own soul also" (Luke 2:22-35).

Satan

Satan, that fallen angel, the prince of darkness, had known Christ was coming ever since the garden of Eden (Genesis 3:15). He undoubtedly looked to Christ's coming with fear and trembling. He knew all too well Christ's mission was to destroy his hold over mankind.

As he faced Christ in the desert he employed every device of darkness available to assist him as he engaged in the greatest battle of all time. "If thou be the Son of God, command that these stones be made bread. . . If thou be the Son of God, cast thyself down: for it is written, "He shall give his angels charge concerning thee: and in their hands they shall bear thee up, lest at any time thou dash thy foot against a stone. . . All these things will I give thee, if thou wilt fall down and worship me" (Matthew 4:1-11).

John the Baptist

John recognized the fact that Christ had come to take away man's sins. "The next day John seeth Jesus coming unto him, and saith, 'Behold the Lamb of God, which taketh away the sin of the world' " (John 1:29).

John knew that although his own earthly age was greater than Christ's, Christ had existed before him. "This is he of whom I said, 'After me cometh a man which is preferred before me: for he was before me' " (John 1:30).

John understood Jesus to be God's son. "And I saw, and bare record that this is the Son of God" (John 1:34).

John knew that Jesus must take preeminence over him. John understood that his mission was to prepare the way for Christ. "Ye yourselves bear me witness, that I said, 'I am not the Christ, but that I am sent before him.' He must increase, but I must decrease" (John 3:28,30).

John also recognized that Jesus came from heaven with heaven's message. "He that cometh from above is above all: he that is of the earth is earthly, and speaketh of the earth: he that cometh from heaven is above all. And what he hath seen and heard, that he testifieth; and no man receiveth his testimony" (John 3:31-32).

He understood that Christ's message was from God and that He had the Spirit without measure. "For he whom God hath sent speaketh the words of God: for God giveth not the Spirit by measure unto him" (John 3:34).

The Adulterous Samaritan Woman and Other Samaritans

Because of her conversation with Jesus this woman was convinced He was the Christ. "Come, see a man, which told me all things that ever I did: is not this the Christ?" (John 4:29). Her question, is not this the Christ, should not be interpreted as indicative of her ignorance but rather as a rhetorical question whose answer is obvious. As a result of her testimony others were interested in finding out more. "Then they went out of the city, and came unto him" (John 4:30). As a matter of fact, many believed solely on this woman's testimony without having to investigate further. "And many of the Samaritans of that city believed on him for the saying of the woman, which testified, 'He told me all that ever I did' " (John 4:39).

Christ stayed for two days and many more believed on him because of the words he spoke. "So when the Samaritans were come unto him, they besought him that he would tarry with them: and he abode there two days. And many more believed because of his word" (John 4:40-41). They saw Him as the Saviour of the world. "And said unto the woman, 'Now we believe, not because of thy saying: for we have heard ourselves, and know that this is indeed the Christ, the Saviour of the world' " (John 4:42).

Two points worthy of note concerning these people are, these people believed without evidence of miracles, but believed based on His teachings. Also, here are Samaritans, despised by the Jewish people, eagerly accepting the Christ.

Demons

"And there was in their synagogue a man with an unclean spirit; and he cried out, saying, 'Let us alone; what have we to do with thee, thou Jesus of Nazareth? art thou come to destroy us? I know thee who thou art, the Holy One of God' " (Mark 1:21-28).

"And when he went forth to land, there met him out of the city a certain man, which had devils long time, and wore no clothes, neither abode in any house, but in the tombs. When he saw Jesus, he cried out, and fell down before him, and with a loud voice said, 'What have I to do with thee, Jesus, thou Son of God most high? I beseech thee, torment me not' (Luke 8:26-39).

Demons recognized Jesus as the Son of God come down from heaven. They knew His mission was to destroy evil, which they represented.

They knew Christ had power over their master—Satan. They understood that He could send them back to the deep, or torments.

The Sinful Woman

This is the woman who wiped Jesus' feet with her hair and anointed them with oil (Luke 7:36-50). At what point this woman came to believe in Jesus we do not know. Perhaps she had been following afar off for some time witnessing His miracles and listening to His message. She saw Jesus as He who is worthy of the highest honor and deepest service capable of mankind. She recognized Him as worthy of worship.

The Multitude At Capernaum

In John 6 we read of a group of people who saw Jesus for who He truly was. They saw that His mission was not physical but spiritual. "Labour not for the meat which perisheth, but for that meat which endureth unto everlasting life, which the son of man shall give unto you: for him hath God the Father sealed" (v. 27). They found out that Jesus would not work a miracle just for spectacle. "They said therefore unto him, 'What sign shewest thou then, that we may see, and believe thee? what doest thou work? Our fathers did eat manna in the desert; as it is written, "He gave them bread from heaven to eat." ' Then Jesus said unto them, 'Verily, verily, I say unto you, Moses gave you that bread from heaven; but my Father giveth you the true bread from heaven. For the bread of God is he which cometh down from heaven and giveth life unto the world' " (vs. 30-33). They saw that Jesus was of the Father and that to get to the Father one had to accept Christ.

Because they saw Jesus so clearly they rejected Him. "From that time many of his disciples went back, and walked no more with him" (v. 66). Christ was not what they wanted Him to be.

The Man Born Blind

In John 9 we read of Jesus healing a man which was blind from his birth. Through subsequent questioning by the Pharisees we learn that this man recognized Christ as being from God. He knew that His power had to be from God. He worshipped Him as God's son.

"Therefore said some of the Pharisees, 'This man is not of God, because he keepeth not the sabbath day.' Others said, 'How can a man that is a sinner do such miracles?' And there was a division among them.

They say unto the blind man again, 'What sayest thou of him, that he hath opened thine eyes?' He said, 'He is a prophet' (vs. 16-17).

"Then they reviled him, and said, 'Thou art his disciple; but we are Moses' disciples. We know that God spake unto Moses: as for this fellow, we know not from whence he is.' The man answered and said unto them, 'Why herein is a marvellous thing, that ye know not from whence he is, and yet he hath opened mine eyes. . . If this man were not of God, he could do nothing' " (vs. 28-33).

Mary and Martha

In John 11 we find the record of the death of Lazarus and Jesus' subsequent journey to Bethany to raise him from the grave. Mary and Martha recognized Jesus' power over sickness. "Therefore his sisters sent unto him, saying, 'Lord, behold, he whom thou lovest is sick!. . . Then said Martha unto Jesus, 'Lord, if thou hadst been here, my brother had not died!. . . Then when Mary was come where Jesus was, and saw him, she fell down at his feet, saying unto him, 'Lord, if thou hadst been here, my brother had not died' " (vs. 3, 21, 32.).

These sisters knew that Christ's power was from God. "But I know, that even now, whatsoever thou wilt ask of God, God will give it thee" (v. 22).

They saw that he was the Christ, the prophecied one, God's son. "Yea, Lord: I believe that thou art the Christ, the Son of God, which should come into the world" (v. 27).

Rich Young Ruler

Based on what this young man had seen or heard, he knew that Jesus had the answer to life's most important question, "What shall I do that I may inherit eternal life?" (Matthew 19:16-22). But Jesus' answer to him was not what he expected. Jesus told this young man that He demanded total allegiance. This the young man could not accept.

How sad that this young man knew Jesus had the answer to eternal life but he would not accept the answer.

Some Rulers of the Jews

"Nevertheless among the chief rulers also many believed on him; but because of the Pharisees they did not confess him, lest they should be put out of the synagogue: for they loved the praise of men more than the praise of God" (John 12:42-43).

A significant point is that the text says "many" not just a few believed. These men were knowledgeable enough in the scriptures to know that based on Jesus' works He had to be the Christ. But their knowledge or faith profited them nothing. This passage speaks strongly about the doctrine of "faith only."

The Apostles

Much time was spent in chapter one discussing the point that the twelve did not see Jesus as He really was. It was not until after His resurrection and hearing His explanation of scriptures that they came to a fuller understanding of His true nature. To get a proper understanding of how Christ taught them and the result it brought about in the lives of the twelve, let's look at the last days of Christ in chronological order.

"Then the eleven disciples went away into Galilee, into a mountain where Jesus had appointed them. And when they saw him, they worshipped him: but some doubted. And Jesus came and spake unto them, saying, 'All power is given unto me in heaven and in earth. Go ye therefore, and teach all nations, baptizing them in the name of the Father and of the Son, and of the Holy Ghost: teaching them to observe all things whatsoever I have commanded you: and, lo, I am with you always, even unto the end of the world' " (Matthew 28:16-20). "And he said unto them, 'Go ye into all the world, and preach the gospel to every creature. He that believeth and is baptized shall be saved; but he that believeth not shall be damned. And these signs shall follow them that believe; in my name shall they cast out devils; they shall speak with new tongues; they shall take up serpents; and if they drink any deadly thing, it shall not hurt them; they shall lay hands on the sick, and they shall recover" (Mark 16:15-18). These two passages, along with a comment by Paul in 1 Corinthians 15:6, are parallel passages referring to Christ's appearance to the 500 with a commission given.

"And he said unto them, 'These are the words which I spake unto you, while I was yet with you, that all things must be fulfilled, which were written in the law of Moses, and in the prophets, and in the psalms, concerning me.' Then opened he their understanding, that they might understand the scriptures, and said unto them, 'Thus it is written, and thus it behoved Christ to suffer, and to rise from the dead the third day: and that repentance and remission of sins should be preached in his name among all nations, beginning at Jerusalem. And ye are witnesses of these things. And, behold, I send the promise of my Father upon you: but tarry ye in the city of Jerusalem, until ye be endued with power from on high' " (Luke 24:44-49). "To whom also he shewed himself alive after his passion by many infallible proofs, being seen of them forty days, and speaking of the things pertaining to the kindgom of God: and, being assembled together with them, commanded them that they should not depart from Jerusalem, 'but wait for the promise of the Father, which,' saith he, 'ye have heard of me. For John truly baptized with water; but ye shall be baptized with the Holy Ghost not many days hence.' When they therefore were come together, they asked of him, saying, 'Lord, wilt thou at this time restore again the kingdom to Israel?' And he said unto them, 'It is not for you to know the times or the seasons, which the Father hath put in his own power. But ye shall receive power, after that the Holy Ghost is come upon you: and ye shall be witness unto me both in Jerusalem, and in all Judea, and in Samaria, and unto the uttermost part of the earth' " (Acts 1:3-8). These are also parallel passages referring to instructions given to the twelve in Jerusalem. How often during this explanation must the disciples have looked at one another and said things like: "Of course! Now I see!" "How foolish of us to not understand sooner!" "Master will you forgive us for being so feeble in our faith?" Christ gave them further instruction concerning the nature of His kingdom and its importance.

"So then after the Lord had spoken unto them, he was received up into heaven, and sat on the right hand of God" (Mark 16:19). "And he led them out as far as Bethany, and he lifted up his hands, and blessed them. And it came to pass, while he blessed them, he was parted from them, and carried up into heaven" (Luke 24:50-51). "And when he had spoken these things, while they beheld, he was taken up; and a cloud received him out of their sight. And while they looked stedfastly toward heaven as he went up, behold, two men stood by them in white apparel; which also said, 'Ye men of Galilee, why stand ye gazing up into heaven? this same Jesus, which is taken up from you into heaven shall so come in like manner as ye have seen him go into heaven" (Acts 1:9-11). Here we read of Christ's last appearance and ascension.

Acts 1:12; Luke 24:52-53; and Mark 16:20 give us an epilogue as to the impact this understanding of the true nature of Christ and His mission had on the twelve. "Then returned they unto Jerusalem from the mount called Olivet, which is from Jerusalem a sabbath days journey." "And they worshipped him, and returned to Jerusalem with great joy: and were continually in the temple, praising and blessing God." "And they went forth, and preached everywhere, the Lord working with them, and confirming the word with signs following."

The apostles worshipped Him now, whereas immediately following Christ's crucifixion they were unsure who to worship. They were now joyful, whereas earlier they thought all reason for joy and hope w-

gone. They now realized their life's mission must be the carrying forth the message of Christ, whereas earlier they knew not what they were going to do with their lives.

Conclusion

There were two kinds of people who saw the true nature of Christ and His mission. One kind were those who were eager to find the Christ but had their own idea of what being a disciple of His would involve. They saw, but Christ demanded so much they would not follow. How sad and tragic that these people recognized the true nature of Christ, believed on Him, but would not act on their faith. They were so close to the kingdom but would not open the door.

Then there were those who accepted Christ and His mission with open hearts. These people changed their lives to pattern after His. They took His nature and made it theirs. And what a change it wrought! Look at the twelve, feebly following Christ during His ministry, barely understanding the meaning of His teachings. After His arrest and crucifixion they are as blind men, wandering with no direction to their lives. Then, after coming to a fuller understanding of Christ and His mission, they march forth to conquer the world for Him! May we follow their footsteps!

Lesson #11

Locate Where They Are Found

1. "Come, see a man, which told me all things that ever I did: is not this the Christ?" ____________________
2. "Why herein is a marvellous thing, that ye know not from whence he is, and yet he hath opened mine eyes." ____________________
3. "Behold this child is set for the fall and rising again of many in Israel." ____________________
4. And they went forth, and preached everywhere. ____________________
5. "Yea, Lord: I believe that thou art the Christ, the Son of God, which should come into the world." ____________________
6. Nevertheless among the chief rulers also many believed on him. ____________________
7. "All these things will I give thee, if thou wilt fall down and worship me." ____________________

8. "Let us alone, what have we to do with thee, thou Jesus of Nazareth?" ____________

9. "And I saw, and bare record that this is the Son of God." ____________

10. And they worshipped him, and returned to Jerusalem with great joy. ____________

Thought Questions

1. Why do you suppose it was often the sinful and oppressed people that saw and accepted Christ so readily, as in John 4 and Luke 7? ____________

2. Enumerate some of the things the people saw concerning Christ, His nature and mission. ____________

3. Can you draw a parallel between what happened to the Twelve after they "saw" Jesus and what should happen to us when we "see" Jesus? ____________

4. Is it enough to acknowledge Jesus as the Son of God? ____________

5. What is the sad part concerning the rich young ruler in Matthew 19 and the rulers of the Jews in John 12? ____________

Chapter 12

THE FACES OF JESUS

For the past 1,400 or more years artists of every nationality have been painting portraits of Christ. Each artist had his own idea of what Jesus looked like, the result being that rarely do any of the portraits look alike. There are portraits of Jesus with a beard and without a beard, with long hair and with short hair, with a pale complexion and with a dark complexion, with a thin, frail body and with a strong, robust body.

Let it be made clear that no one knows exactly what Jesus looked like. But because of, I suppose, human nature, everyone has a mental picture of what they think Christ looked like. When you partake of the Lord's supper, or when you pray, or when you study about Christ don't you have a mental picture of what He looks like? Think about it for a moment. And isn't that mental picture always the same? This is a phenomenon familiar to us all.

But I'm not really interested in whether your mental image of Jesus had long hair or short, has a beard or not, has a pale complexion or a dark one. What I want to know is, what kind of expression does He have on His face? When you look closely with your mind's eye to see the detail of His face, what do you see? Maybe you have a hard time fixing a particular expression on Him. Or maybe the expression is always the same.

The expression on a man's face can tell you quite a lot about that man. They tell you how he feels about certain things. They reveal what kinds of things touch him emotionally. They show the range of emotions he possesses. This is very true of Jesus. In this chapter we will notice five different expressions, or faces, of Jesus and see what they reveal to us about Him.

The Face Of Compassion

"And there came a leper to him, beseeching him, and kneeling down to him, and saying unto him, 'If thou wilt, thou canst make me clean.' And Jesus, moved with compassion, put forth his hand, and touched him, and saith unto him, 'I will; be thou clean.' And as soon as he had spoken, immediately the leprosy departed from him, and he was cleansed" (Mark 1:40-42).

This incident was referred to in chapter five. Remember what a contrast there was between Christ and the leper? A diseased man beside one who could heal diseases. A scarred man beside a perfect man. One man kneeling, another standing. One man begging, another granting.

What great faith and hope this man must have had as he "got up the nerve" to approach Christ! For years he had suffered with this sickening and incurable disease of leprosy. All hope had gone from his life until he started hearing of the man called Jesus who had the power to heal all diseases. What joy and hope filled this man's heart as he knelt before the Saviour.

Yet, what great apprehension must have been in his heart! How would this man called Jesus react to him? Were the stories concerning His power over diseases exaggerated? The tales of His great compassion for mankind untrue? What right did he, a leper, have in approaching this one who claimed to be from God? Was he just "fooling himself" in thinking anyone would care about him and his condition?

As this leper knelt before Jesus with fear, hope, and uncertainty in his heart, he slowly lifted his face to look upon this man in whom he had put so much faith. As his eyes met the eyes of the Saviour his heart probably melted with relief as he looked upon the kindest, most compassionate face he had ever seen.

Jesus knew the man's pain and misery and the hope that was in his heart. As he reached out and lovingly touched this man's face perhaps a gentle tear came to our Saviour's eye as His heart went out to this scarred and diseased man.

Oh what a compassionate man was our Saviour!

The Face Of Anger

This is one face of our Saviour that we overlook, maybe intentionally. But be assured, Jesus could be angered. On one occasion, after finding animals being sold and money being exchanged in the temple, He made a scourge of small cords and drove out the sheep, oxen, and money changers. He poured out the changers' money, and overthrew the tables. He was furious! (John 2:13-17).

On another occasion Jesus vented His pent up anger on the scribes and Pharisees. He used words of sarcasm. "Everything they do is done for men to see: They make their phylacteries wide and the tassels of their prayer shawls long; they love the place of honor at banquets and the most important seats in the synagogues; they love to be greeted in the marketplaces and to have men call them 'Rabbi.' "

He used their own teachings to condemn them. "Woe to you, blind guides! You say, 'If anyone swears by the temple, it means nothing; but if anyone swears by the gold of the temple, he is bound by his oath.' You blind fools! Which is greater: the gold, or the temple that makes the gold sacred? You also say, 'If anyone swears by the altar, it means nothing; but if anyone swears by the gift on it, he is bound by his oath.' You blind men! Which is greater: the gift, or the altar that makes the gift sacred? Therefore, he who swears by the temple swears by it and by the one who dwells in it. And he who swears by heaven swears by God's throne and by the one who sits on it."

Christ ridicules them. "Woe to you, teachers of the law and Pharisees, you hypocrites! You are like whitewashed tombs, which look beautiful on the outside but on the inside are full of dead men's bones and everything unclean. In the same way, on the outside you appear to people as righteous but on the inside you are full of hypocrisy and wickedness."

Jesus even calls them names. "You snakes! You brood of vipers!" (above passages from Matthew 23 NIV)

The face of Jesus could become dark like a stormcloud and his eyes flash like lightning when provoked by men such as the scribes and Pharisees. Here were people who should have known better, had the opportunity to know better, but openly rebelled against God and His Son.

The Face of Disappointment

In John 6 Christ tells the multitudes following to count the cost of discipleship. He issues what some called "hard saying," that is, they were hard to accept. As a result, "Many of his disciples went back, and walked no more with him."

Imagine the disappointment of Christ as He looked at the departing backs of those who had been following Him. Perhaps He was fighting back tears of disappointment when He turned to the twelve and asked them, "Will ye also go away?"

Luke 22 is the record of the tragic incident of Peter's denial of Christ. "And the Lord said, 'Simon, Simon, behold, Satan hath desired to have you, that he may sift you as wheat: but I have prayed for thee, that thy faith fail not: and when thou art converted, strengthen thy brethren.' And he said unto him, 'Lord, I am ready to go with thee, both into prison, and to death.' And he said, 'I tell thee, Peter, the cock shall not crow this day, before that thou shalt thrice deny that thou knowest me' " (vs. 31-34).

"Then took they him, and led him, and brought him into the high priest's house. And Peter followed afar off. And when they had kindled a fire in the midst of the hall, and were set down together, Peter sat down among them. But a certain maid beheld him as he sat by the fire, and earnestly looked upon him, and said, 'This man was also with him.' And he denied him, saying, 'Woman, I know him not.' And after a little while another saw him, and said, 'Thou art also of them.' And Peter said, 'Man, I am not.' And about the space of one hour after another confidently affirmed, saying, 'Of a truth this fellow also was with him: for he is a Galilaean.' And Peter said, 'Man, I know not what thou sayest.' And immediately, while he yet spake, the cock crew. And the Lord turned, and looked upon Peter. And Peter remembered the word of the Lord how he had said unto him, 'Before the cock crow, thou shalt deny me thrice.' And Peter went out, and wept bitterly" (vs. 54-62).

As that rooster crowed and the crowd parted to where Peter and Jesus' eyes met, what expression do you think Peter saw on the Master's face? No doubt it was a look of bitter disappointment. How would you have felt if you had been Peter and known you had disappointed your precious Saviour? No wonder Peter went out and wept bitterly!

Of course Jesus, being God's son, knew that there would be those who would disappoint Him. But that knowledge did not lessen the sadness it caused him. A parallel can be seen in parents raising their children. They know that at some point their children will disappoint them in some way or another, but that does not lessen the hurt.

The Face Of Pain

How often do we stop to seriously and soberly consider the physical pain endured during His trail and crucifixion? It seems that sometimes we think that because He was God's son He was somehow "above" the pain. But this is not so. Jesus was human *just like* you and me. The pain he felt was real as the pain you and I feel.

The whip that was used during the scourging was an instrument of the utmost cruelty. It was made of several ropes or cords plaited together. On the ends of the unplaited cords which struck the victim were tied bits of sharp bone or metal. The pain was caused not only by the force of the blow but also by the sharp objects ripping and tearing the flesh off the back of the victim. Often a person would die during a scourging due to the loss of blood from its blows. The pain etched on our Saviour's face during His scourging is hard for us to imagine!

Jesus also endured a cruel mocking by the soldiers during one of His examinations. They placed the wicked crown of thorns upon His head and smote Him with the reed. On another occasion they apparently blindfolded and took turns slapping His face and spitting on Him taunting Him to prophecy which one of them had hit Him.

Now we must turn our eyes to Golgotha's cruel hill. Never has a more cruel way of being murdered been imagined by bent and twisted minds than that of crucifixion on a cross. The nails used were not the smooth, sleek kind we have today, but were formed by being hammered out on an anvil. They were bent and twisted, with jagged edges. As the heavy hammer drove them, the flesh would tear and the pain would sear throughout the body. At each blow of the wooden mallet our Saviour's face would writhe in pain and agony. The hollow echo of those blows echo through time pain unimaginable!

This scene is so hard for us to behold that we turn our faces quickly away.

The Face Of Sorrow

In John 11 we read of the passing of Jesus' dear friend Lazarus. When Lazarus fell sick, his sisters, Mary and Martha, sent word to Jesus to come. After waiting a couple of days, He journeyed to Bethany. In the meantime Lazarus had died. "And many of the Jews came to Martha and Mary, to comfort them concerning their brother."

When Martha heard that Jesus was coming, she eagerly ran out to meet Him to receive strength from His presence. After talking with Him and receiving words of hope, she went and told Mary of Jesus' coming. Mary also eagerly ran and fell at His feet to receive words of encouragement.

After talking with these two grief stricken women and seeing the "Jews also weeping which came," the Bible says Jesus "groaned in the spirit." He felt something that reached to the core of His essence. It was a feeling that could not be verbally expressed. Have you ever been to a funeral service and heard a close loved one of the deceased, in deep sorrow, utter a sound that was not a cry or anything but that which could be described as a groan? Such was the sound our Lord made on this occasion. And as the procession arrived at the sealed grave, Jesus was overcome and wept! What a wonderfully touching scene!

Conclusion

These five faces of Jesus, the face of compassion, the face of anger, the face of disappointment, the face of pain, and the face of sorrow were expressions of His during His earthly ministry. But if we could part the curtain into heaven and look upon His face again, we would undoubtedly see the same expressions today. Surely there is sorrow on His face over those who die almost persuaded to be one of His children. No doubt He has a face of pain when His followers bring shame on Him and His church. The Hebrew writer says it is just like crucifying Him afresh (Hebrews 6:6). If we could see Jesus' face today there would be times we would see a face of disappointment as people have an opportunity to take a Christian stand but turn away. We can be sure His face darkens in anger toward those who know the truth but are openly rebellious. But we should be most thankful that He still has the face of compassion. He is longsuffering toward us. He is not willing that any should perish. He is ready to welcome all with open arms.

Lesson #12
Locate Where They Are Found

1. "Woe unto you, ye blind guides." ________________
2. And the Lord turned, and looked upon Peter. . . And Peter went out, and wept bitterly. ________________
3. Then said Jesus unto the twelve, "Will ye also go away?" ________________
4. When Jesus therefore saw her weeping, and the Jews also weeping which came with her, he groaned in the spirit, and was troubled. ________________
5. "Woe unto you, scribes and Pharisees, hypocrites!" ________________
6. And the men that held Jesus mocked him, and smote him. ________________
7. Jesus wept. ________________
8. "Ye blind guides, which strain at a gnat, and swallow a camel." ________________

9. And Jesus, moved with compassion, put forth his hand, and touched him. ______

10. From that time many of his disciples went back, and walked no more with him. ______

Thought Questions

1. From looking at or picturing these expressions on the face of Jesus, what do you feel you learned about Him? ______

2. Which face do we try not to see and why is this so? ______

3. Which expression do you think Jesus has on His face when He looks at your life? ______

4. How can we crucify Jesus today? ______

5. Give examples of how we can cause each of these expressions today. ______

Chapter 13

WHAT HAVE YOU SEEN?

In this study of the life of Christ my purpose has been to help you see more clearly the true nature of Christ and His mission. In reality, the study of the life of Christ is a life-long study. The longer and deeper one looks the more one sees. The book has only touched the hem of the garment. Hopefully you have been motivated to study His life more closely.

I have made a conscious effort to challenge the reader to compare what he sees in Christ's life to what he sees in his own life. We all must examine our lives closely and see how "Christ-like" we really are. The most profitable studies are those which bring about a change of life on the part of the student. I trust this has been the case for you as it was for me. If we don't use our better understanding of the nature of Christ by applying this knowledge to our lives, then we put ourselves in the same class as those rulers of the Jews in John 12:42-43.

Now, as we come to the end of this study, let's look back and try to get a composite look at the man, Jesus.

In chapter one we noted some of the aspects of Christ that are central to His nature and mission. Christ is all-powerful. He demonstrated power over nature through calming the sea. He showed power over disease by healing the sick and lame. His power over death was seen in His raising people from the dead. He forgave people of their sins.

Christ had to suffer and die. It was part of the cost to be paid. He deserves to be treated with the utmost honor and respect. He was a servant to others and told them to go and do likewise. He told others that His kingdom was not an earthly one but heavenly.

The sad note was that these very traits were the ones that caused the world to reject Him.

In chapter two we saw Jesus helping people set priorities in their lives.

He constantly emphasized the importance everyone needs to place on spiritual things. He belittled the importance of physical things. A great contrast to the thinking of the world.

Christ stressed that if we focused more on the hearts of men and affected a change there, then a proper way of life will come about.

It was in chapter three that we studied the attitudes of humility and a spirit of service. Christ showed that when one is humble he will be eager to serve and when one serves others it will make him humble. He taught we should not desire to always be in a position of giving orders and being served by others. But rather, the true end of the servant of God is to serve, not to be served. We should never feel we are "too good" to perform any service for our fellow man.

The wonderful spirit of compassion demonstrated by Christ was studied in chapter four. In observing Jesus, we saw people of varying backgrounds eagerly respond to Him because He reached out to them first with compassion. People were drawn to His compassionate spirit like a magnet. Never had they experienced such!

Jesus' compassionate spirit was an integral part of His nature that affected His every dealing with man. It was not just a feeling but an attitude that manifested itself in actions.

It was in chapter five that we saw Jesus dealing with individuals with misguided zeal. Jesus taught clearly that knowledge must temper our zeal. Our zeal toward wiping out sin must not cause us to hate sinners themselves. The reason Jesus came to earth was to seek and save the lost. And that is the same purpose we have.

The apostles were those who allowed their misguided zeal to cause them to have a vengeful attitude. It was an attitude that if one was not willing to accept the truth at once he should be destroyed.

We must remember that prayer, patience, and mercy will help us win others to Christ.

In chapter six we looked at a side of Christ that we sometimes don't want to see, the side of anger. Jesus' wrath seemed to be kindled by five types of people: (1) those not prepared to receive Him even though they have been given ample opportunity to prepare; (2) those who refused to believe in Him even in the face of indisputable testimony; (3) those who looked too much on the outward man and too little on the inward man; (5) those who lacked a proper understanding of the importance of extending grace toward others. We must take care that we do not anger Jesus by falling into one of these five categories.

Then in chapter seven we tried to see what Jesus taught concerning our relationship with the world. One striking thing we saw was that Jesus went right into the midst of sinners. He showed them He cared about them as a person. He accepted them where they were at that point in their life. Then he challenged them to take up a more noble cause, that of following Him.

Jesus places great importance on the souls of lost individuals. To Him one soul is not more important than another. He looks more at what a person can become, through Him, than at what he is.

We must reach out to the world as friendly, compassionate, and interested people if we expect to convert others.

We looked in chapter eight at the importance Christ places on counting the cost of discipleship and what that cost involves. Christ never deceived anyone into thinking that it would be easy to follow Him. He wants our whole life, not just part of it. This involves being willing to: (1) serve others; (2) sever ties with family, friends, occupation, social activities; (3) suffer persecutions; (4) sacrifice anything and everything; (5) accept Christ as a way of life; (6) bear fruit.

In chapter nine we asked the important question, what are you doing for Christ? We looked at different scenes where Christ revealed what acts of service He considered to be worthy of praise. From these scenes we learned that He is interested more in the quality of our service to Him than He is in the quantity of our service. He is concerned about what motivates us to serve Him. Is it love, devotion, and gratitude? or is it the praise of others, personal satisfaction, or material gain?

Christ teaches we should expect to do great service for Him. That is why we are saved. It is our vocation.

As we came to chapter ten we tried to learn from Jesus the value of touching people where they hurt. Christ cultivated the hearts of the people by showing them He cared enough about them to help them. Curing their physical ills opened their spiritual hearts. Their response to Him was to eagerly listen to His words of hope and comfort for their spiritual ills. How much we need to learn this important point!

In chapter eleven we took a look at those individuals who seemed to have a clearer understanding of the nature of Christ and His mission. Some people saw Him and as a result rejected Him. Others saw Him and gladly received Him into their hearts.

In the apostles we saw that when people understand the true mission of Christ and His nature and they readily accept Him, it results in a transformation of their life.

In chapter twelve we endeavored to study very closely the nature of the man, Jesus, by looking at the expression on His face. There we saw compassion, anger, disappointment, pain, and sorrow.

Conclusion

Have you really seen Jesus? Has He made a difference in your way of living?

He was truly Divinity clothed in a human tabernacle.

His nature is multifaceted like a polished gem. When we think we see Him completely, we look closer and find something more beautiful and challenging.

Christ came to earth to reveal God and His message to man. This He did in word and deed.

Let us ever strive to pattern our lives more nearly like His.

And let us ever hold up Christ before the world and plead for others to come to Him.

Lesson #13

Thought Questions

1. Which of the lessons studied hit closest to you? Why? _______________

   ____

2. Which of the lessons do you think you as a congregation need to work harder at applying? Why? ____________________________________

   ____

3. Since you have been studying these lessons have you noted a change in yourself and the other members of your class? _____________________

   ____

4. What do you think is the most striking characteristic of Christ? (one that stands out above the others) ________________________________

   ____

5. How can we motivate others to live a more Christ-like life? ____________

   ____